Facets of Domestication

DIS/CONTINUITIES

TORUŃ STUDIES IN LANGUAGE, LITERATURE AND CULTURE

Edited by Mirosława Buchholtz

Advisory Board
Leszek Berezowski (Wroclaw University)
Annick Duperray (University of Provence)
Dorota Guttfeld (Nicolaus Copernicus University)
Grzegorz Koneczniak (Nicolaus Copernicus University)
Piotr Skrzypczak (Nicolaus Copernicus University)
Jordan Zlatev (Lund University)

Vol. 10

PETER LANG
EDITION

Dorota Guttfeld (ed.)

Facets of Domestication

Case Studies in Polish-English and English-Polish Translation

PETER LANG
EDITION

Bibliographic Information published by the Deutsche Nationalbibliothek
The Deutsche Nationalbibliothek lists this publication in the Deutsche
Nationalbibliografie; detailed bibliographic data is available in the internet
at http://dnb.d-nb.de.

Library of Congress Cataloging-in-Publication Data
Facets of domestication : case studies in Polish-English and English-Polish
translation / Dorota Guttfeld (ed.).
    pages cm. – (Dis/Continuities Toruń Studies in language, literature and
culture ; v. 10)
  Includes bibliographical references.
  ISBN 978-3-631-66065-2 (Print) – ISBN 978-3-653-05412-5 (E-Book)
  1. Translating and interpreting–Study and teaching–Case studies.
2. Translating and interpreting–Poland–Case studies. 3. English language–
Translations into Polish–Case studies. 4. Polish language–Translations into
English–Case studies. I. Guttfeld, Dorota, editor.
  P306.5.F33 2015
  491.8'580221–dc23
                              2015018846

This publication was financially supported by
the Nicolaus Copernicus University, Toruń.

ISSN 2193-4207
ISBN 978-3-631-66065-2 (Print)
E-ISBN 978-3-653-05412-5 (E-Book)
DOI 10.3726/978-3-653-05412-5

© Peter Lang GmbH
Internationaler Verlag der Wissenschaften
Frankfurt am Main 2015
All rights reserved.
Peter Lang Edition is an Imprint of Peter Lang GmbH.

Peter Lang – Frankfurt am Main · Bern · Bruxelles ·
New York · Oxford · Warszawa · Wien

This publication has been peer reviewed.

www.peterlang.com

Table of contents

Dorota Guttfeld
Facets of domestication 7

English to Polish: the protective translator

Joanna Szakiel
Translation and ideology. His Holiness John Paul II and the
hidden history of our times in Polish 13

Ewa Tadajewska
Domestication and foreignization in children's literature.
Culture-specific items in two Polish translations of Anne
of Green Gables 35

Polish to English: the exotic East

Karolina Retkowska
Old Polish attire in English. Foreignness and domesticity
in the English translations of Adam Mickiewicz's Pan Tadeusz..........................49

Krzysztof Wadyński
From the Wild Fields to the DVD. A domesticating
approach in the translation of With Fire and Sword 73

Natalia Grabowska
From the Orient Westwards. Cultural items in two
English translations of Sonety krymskie by Adam Mickiewicz 89

Polish and English: between translation and adaptation

Joanna Szakiel
Two audiences, two messages. A case study of
self-translation in Fear / Strach by Jan Tomasz Gross 111

Aleksandra Borowska
Localizing a new text-type. Anglophone Internet memes
and their Polish versions 131

Dominika Grygowska
Humour and cultural references in constrained translation.
The Polish translation of Munchkin, a non-collectible card game 151

Contributors.. 177

Facets of domestication

The present volume is a collection of papers based on the B.A. and M.A. projects of translation studies graduates from the Department of English at Nicolaus Copernicus University in Toruń, Poland. The findings from these diploma theses all illustrate various degrees of the source texts' adaptation to target culture standards. The common denominator is the authors' engagement with the concept of domestication.

Lawrence Venuti, who rediscovered the term for translation studies, argues that "every act of translating wreaks on a foreign text" some form of "ethnocentric violence" which ought, for ideological reasons, be countermanded "by a violent disruption of domestic values that challenges cultural forms of domination, whether nationalist or elitist" (Venuti 1995: 147), so as to exert "an ethnodeviant pressure on those (cultural) values to register the linguistic and cultural difference of the foreign text" (20).

If the original sin of translation is not redeemed by such efforts at foreignization, the rendering becomes "an ethnocentric reduction of the foreign text to target-language cultural values" (20), a domesticating translation that "masks an insidious domestication of foreign texts, rewriting them in the transparent discourse that prevails in English and that selects precisely those foreign texts amenable to fluent translating" (17).

Since a domesticated text "conforms to values currently dominating the target-language culture, taking a conservative and openly assimilationist approach to the foreign text, appropriating it to support domesticating canons, publishing trends, political alignments" (Venuti 1998: 240), if domestication becomes the accepted norm, it "prevents an engagement with cultural difference because foreign texts, whatever their origin, are uniformly pressed into homely moulds" (Munday 2009: 98).

Although criticized for his, paradoxically, American-centric perspective and elitist attitude to translation and literature as academic natural past-times (see Pym 2010), as well as his combative and unqualified pronouncements, Venuti remains a powerful influence in translation studies (Kearns 2009). One of the initiation rites for many students of translation is facing the proposition that domestication might not be the only way to do translation, and that translation itself is not necessarily an innocent activity, let alone the transparent mediation that many believe it can and should be.

The realization that domesticating translation behaviors are "enforced by editors, publishers, and reviewers" and that the resulting renderings are molded to be "eminently readable and therefore consumable on the book market, assisting in their commodification and insuring the neglect of foreign texts and (...) discourses that are more resistant to easy readability" (Venuti 1995: 16) opens translation studies to the discussion of (cultural) politics, ideology, social attitudes to otherness, reader preferences and horizons of expectations, to use a term borrowed by Meg Brown from reception theory, and (self)fashioning in international relationships.

This volume presents papers by graduates of the Department of English in the Faculty of Languages at the Nicolaus Copernicus University in Toruń, Poland, all based on their B.A. and M.A. research projects in English-Polish and Polish-English translation. For a beginner-scholar, the most obvious way to test Venuti's claims is to research the translation of culture-specific items. More challenging projects include the analysis of stylistic shifts, the rearrangement and manipulation of the content, the application of target-side genre conventions, the selection of texts for translation, or the emergence and formulation of internal translation policies. The study of culture-specific items benefits from various categorizations of procedures (or techniques) used to render them in translation, such as the taxonomies developed by Javier Aixela or Piotr Kwieciński, which are employed in some of the following papers. Kwieciński also introduces a distinction between the procedures themselves, situating them on a spectrum between exoticism and assimilation, and the (domestication or foreignizing) effects they may but do not have to cause. While the two frameworks are closely connected, they need not be synonymous. Since the effects of particular procedures may be assessed from the reactions of the audience, some of the papers included in this volume include attempts at surveying target reader preferences.

The case studies in the first part of the book discuss English-Polish translation. While Venuti initially described domestication as a tendency visible in translations from relatively minor languages into dominant ones, such as (American) English, the section illustrates its appearance in translations into Polish as well. The first paper, by Joanna Szakiel, illustrates the political pressure exerted on the source text in translation, and the uneasy relationship with the foreign: the outsider perspective of the Western journalists on what target readers may view as an essentially Polish specialty is very much welcome, as long as it is flattering and does not contradict the expected notions of decorum, which needs to be protected by means of translation shifts. The next article, by Ewa Tadajewska, illustrates similar shifts in the translation of a literary text; to facilitate identification with the protagonist, her original religious denomination is partially hidden from view of the Polish reader.

The second part of the volume focuses of the ways Polish culture seeks to represent itself to the Western recipient. The texts under analysis include some of the most canonical representations of Polishness. The article by Karolina Retkowska discusses the icon of the Sarmatian nobleman, transported West by the rather domesticating renderings of traditional Polish attire. Krzysztof Wadyński examines culture-specific items (notably forms of address and elements of material culture) universalized in the translation of a film based on one of the most influential Polish novels, depicting a mythologized period of heroic struggle. Natalia Grabowska views Poland's own complex relationship with the East as the source of this crucial sense of exoticism, and studies English translations of Oriental terminology in some of the most famous Polish poetry.

The three articles featured in the last part of the book investigate less traditional cases of interlingual transfer. Joanna Szakiel discusses a fascinating case of self-translation in another study of a non-fiction book, illustrating the influence of the target readership, the communicative situation, and the cultural context in which a text is to be received on its form and content. Aleksandra Borowska examines the propagation of viral pictures on the Internet as a chance to witness the emergence of new genres and translation norms. Dominika Grygowska analyses translators' priorities in rendering cultural references and humour in the Polish version of a card game, and notes the growing influence of globalization on the margin of freedom the translators are allowed to enjoy.

I hope that the papers showcase the variety of research topics available to young researchers, inspire further studies in the field, and encourage younger students to pursue their interest in translation. I would like to thank the Head of the Department of English as well as the Dean of the Faculty of Languages for making this variety possible, and for their support of this publication.

Dorota Guttfeld

References

Kearns, John. 2009. "Strategies" in Mona Baker and Gabriela Saldanha (eds.), *Routledge Encyclopedia of Translation Studies*. London / New York: Routledge, 282–285.

Munday, Jeremy. 2009. *Routledge companion to translation studies*. London / New York: Routledge.

Pym, Anthony. 2010. *Venuti's visibility*. http://usuaris.tinet.cat/apym/on-line/translation/1996_Venuti.pdf, DOA April 1, 2015.

Venuti, Lawrence. 1995. *The translator's invisibility: a history of translation*. London / New York: Routledge.

Venuti, Lawrence. 1998. "Strategies of translation" in Mona Baker and Kirsten Malmkjaer (eds.) *Routledge Encyclopedia of Translation Studies*. London / New York: Routledge, 240–244.

English to Polish:
the protective translator

Joanna Szakiel

Translation and ideology.
His Holiness John Paul II and the hidden history of our times in Polish

(Re)imaging the pope

John Paul II is considered one of the most prominent and influential people of the past century, and certainly one of the most internationally recognizable Poles. Credited with a substantial contribution to the fall of the Iron Curtain and the renewal of the dialogue between Catholicism and Judaism, the pope was perceived by many not only as a religious leader but an important figure in the global political arena. The first non-Italian in over 400 years, the most-travelled and polyglot pontiff, he focused international attention fostered by extensive media coverage.

In Poland, John Paul II is a commonly respected national symbol of over-throwing Soviet control and the emergence of the Solidarity movement. Within a spiritual dimension, the paternal attitude of Karol Wojtyła was associated with integrity and strength. The pope's visits to his homeland gathered millions of Poles, causing national euphoria. John Paul II became the patron of innumerable public organizations and institutions, and his birthplace, Wadowice, a destination of pilgrimages from all over the country.

For the purpose of illustrating the manner in which the Polishness of 'JP II' and his influence on the nation's history and culture are emphasized, the article written upon JP II's death by one of Poland's leading politicians, Radek Sikorski, can serve as an exceptionally representative example. Sikorski's article "The Pope as Pole" (2005) inscribes into a poetics presenting John Paul II as a "father", "guardian angel", "pastor to the world" and generally evoking associations with heroism, passion and holiness. Sikorski praises the pope's ability to raise hope and pride in the nation, his supportive involvement in Wałęsa's initiative and the ultimate fall of communism in Poland; interestingly, he perceives an analogous link between the pope's 2001 trip to the Ukraine and the subsequent Orange Revolution. The former deputy foreign minister of Poland and the ED of the New Atlantic Initiative at the time of publishing the article (since 2007 Sikorski has been Poland's Minister of Foreign Affairs and the Speaker of the Sejm) does not hide his emotional attachment to Karol Wojtyła. Sikorski's article is filled with the atmosphere of mysticism, the pope is ascribed the attributes of saint-hood and prophecy, described as "national redeemer" (44), "the king" (44), and compared to Moses, who "led us across the Red Sea into the land of liberty and democracy" (45).

The foremost question the paper seeks to address is whether it is possible for a translator to remain neutral given the exceptionally high profile the Polish pontiff enjoys in his homeland and to what degree the conditioning ideological framework affects translation choices. In June 1997 *Gazeta Wyborcza* published an article "Amberyzacja Jego Świątobliwości" by Tomasz Mirkowicz, in which the journalist criticises the Polish translation of Carl Bernstein and Marco Politi's *His Holiness John Paul II and the Hidden History of Our Times* by Stanisław Głąbiński. Mirkowicz enumerates several dozen of the most striking translation shifts. His observations served as the starting point for a detailed analysis for the sake of this paper, which seeks to present them in the light of the concepts of patronage and poetics. The examination encompassed: the treatment of cultural elements in the book (using terminology developed by Kwieciński in *Disturbing Strangeness* to assess whether the translation seems to lean towards domestication or foreignization); the rendition of religious lexical items; cases of ennoblement (to use Berman's term for one of "deforming tendencies" in translation) involving the style as well as content of the book; and the most interesting cases of translation shifts in general.

Translation, history and culture

Research on translation from a cultural perspective is designated by Lefevere and Bassnett as potentially the most profitable development for translation studies (1992a: 10). They state that culturally-oriented analysis should take into consideration such aspects as text type or register, and be closely related to "ideology" and "poetics". The focus on manipulative processes determined by the prevailing ideology or poetics suggests the perception of translation as "one of the strategies cultures develop to deal with what lies outside their boundaries (…) – the kind of strategy that ultimately belongs to the realm of change and survival, not in dictionaries and grammars" (10). Accordingly, the study of translation should not concentrate on the linguistic level but rather redirect its focus onto socio-cultural dimension, and an acute awareness of the complexity and distinctiveness of foreign context is to be regarded as a prerequisite for translators. (Lefevere 1992a: 59)

Translation is seen as a channel through which cultural influences are transferred. Treating translations as a form of manipulation, Lefevere (1992a: xi) indicates two possible ramifications of rewriting: enrichment or impoverishment of the target culture text, literature and society. In the first case, the target audience is supplied with innovative literary types and devices, in the latter, however, it is not only prevented from benefiting from such alternatives, but also presented with deceptive models.

In "The role of ideology in the shaping of translation", Lefevere highlights the socio-economic relations conditioning translators' conduct. One of decisive factors in shaping ideology is the presence and identity of patrons, namely those who commission or publish translations or, in other words, constitute "the link between the translator's text and the audience the translator wants to reach" (6). Owing to their inferior position, the translators are unable to reach the intended audience, unless they comply with their patrons' recommendations.

The last decade of the 20ᵗʰ century saw many scholars remaining unconvinced about the new approach. In 1992 Lefevere published three books advocating the cultural turn in translation studies and, together with Bassnett, came to be credited with the major contribution to the development of cultural perspective. The main assumptions enumerated in one of those books, *Translation, rewriting and the manipulation of literary frame*, including the role of ideology, poetics and patronage as factors controlling the literary system, will be applied in the case study.

Factors controlling the literary system

Lefevere observes that "literature is not a deterministic concept" (1992b: 12), as it is itself subjected to control by numerous factors. He enumerates three major types of such factors. Translated literature functions within the borders of a literary system subordinated to the influence of professional readership, the dominant "poetics" as well as "patronage".

The group of professional readers comprises people who are professionally connected to translated literature, as opposed to those who "do not read literature as written by its writers, but as written by its rewriters" (4). Thus, the category primarily includes literary critics, teachers, reviewers and translators. (1992b: 13–14) Conceived of as "power in the Foucauldian sense" (15), "patronage" denotes people and institutions operating mainly outside the literary system. According to Lefevere, it is the conditioning framework of ideology rather than poetics that constitutes its main point of reference.

Patronage can be commanded by individuals (influential authorities, prominent political figures) as well as groups of people (the media, publishers, religious bodies, political parties etc.) who control the relationship between literary and other cultural systems. The coordination is maintained at institutional level through regulatory agencies managing literary distribution, such as censorship, critical journals and educational organizations. What is more, the constellation of ideological assumptions underlying patronage's treatment of its subordinates frequently coincides with the convictions of those professionals who support the models occupying the central position in the literary polysystem or, as Lefevere terms it, advocate "reigning orthodoxy" (15). (1992b: 15–18)

Lefevere (1992b: 16) distinguishes three, not necessarily correlating, manifestations of patronage: based on ideology, economy and status. The ideological element governs the selection of texts and their marketing. Lefevere places this process within general, ideological borders not restricted to politics. The self-explanatory economic facet concerns remuneration paid to patrons' subordinates and due to its hierarchical structure is usually closely tied with commercial exigencies of the publishing industry. Finally, the status element applies to various ways of imposing the patron's constellation of principles upon a subordinate. Compliance with the regulations observed by patrons and adoption of an attitude pursuant to their expectations results in integration with a group or society perceived as prestigious.

Culture-specific lexical elements

A translated text is a product of an agent subjected to all kinds of political, ethical and economic restraints imposed by the society in which s/he functions. Therefore, translation is, by its very nature, an ideological construct. The first area where the translator's stance may be visible is the treatment of culture-specific items.

Piotr Kwieciński systematized the taxonomy of translation procedures concerning cultural items by gathering and juxtaposing procedural classifications proposed by numerous theoreticians. In *Disturbing Strangeness* he proposes a consolidated arrangement, progressive in terms of domestication, of foreignizing and domesticating strategies. It is important to note that, although Venuti's concepts of domestication and foreignization are adopted by many scholars (the former term referring to protectiveness towards TT context, the latter to more faithful and therefore challenging renderings), Venuti's advocacy of foreignization is not necessarily valid in cases of translation from (rather than into) a politically dominant language (cf. Hatim and Mason, 1997: 120–121).

Kwieciński's group of foreignizing procedures opens with *transference of images or sounds*, when a sound or image characteristic for a source culture is retained unchanged in the target text. The second procedure, *borrowing*, can be morphologically, phonologically or orthographically adapted, and comprises ad-hoc borrowing, importation, and recent borrowings; it allows for distancing device, such as quotation marks. The third operation, labeled as *calque, coinage, semantic extension* stands for potentially linguistically disruptive calques, neologisms and semantic extensions both ad hoc and recently created; distancing devices are fully applicable as well. Some combinations of these procedures as distinguished by Kwieciński may include intra- or extratextual *glosses*. The procedure referred to as *recognised exoticism* encompasses transmitting specifically SC expressions which, thanks to incorporation of already recognised equivalents in the TC, are relatively understandable to target language users. Built on cultural, political and social discrepancies, recognised exoticism is acknowledged as a partition case between domesticating and foreignizing procedures.

Kwieciński situates normalization, deletion, covert cultural substitution or covert acculturation and covert cultural substitution or covert acculturation within the category of domesticating procedures. *Normalization* involves stylistic, structural and lexical adjustments of SC-specific elements by means of relations extending through both cultures. Its internal division includes: repackaging (diffusion and condensation, implying expansion or condensation of target language counterparts), generalization, specification, modification and mutation (an irreversible process, since the SL concept is modulated to such a degree that the original meaning becomes untraceable). *Deletion* involves the omission of a SC element, often accompanied by various types of compensation procedures. *Covert cultural substitution* involves replacing an item peculiar to the SC with a TC element in a non-evident manner, so that the translational intervention is concealed, while *covert acculturation* signifies the replacement of a transcultural concept by a TC-specific item wihich may go unnoticed by the target reader. By contrast, *overt cultural substitution* refers to those cases where an analogous process is combined with deliberate manifestations of the SC item's otherness, resulting in the translator's visibility; similarly, *overt acculturation* involves the insertion of a specifically TC concept into the target text to replace a transcultural SL item. (Kwieciński 2001: 157–165)

The analysis of the translation of Polish cultural items in Bernstein's and Politi's *His Holiness. John Paul II and the hidden history of our times* shows that the overall tendency is towards normalization. On the tentative axis with borrowing at one, and overt cultural substitution at the other extreme, the procedures used can be placed closer to the latter, as manifestations of domesticating mechanisms. Normalization, however, in this case is not to be understood in its strict sense, since an appreciable majority of the examined lexical elements derive from domestic, Polish context. That the "cultural narcissism" (Venuti 1998: 20) of the English language is not augmented here is not necessarily a result of the translator's global choice, but rather seems to derive from the fact that the lexical culture-specific elements are chiefly "re-embedded" into the Polish context.

More specifically, among normalising procedures, semantic and stylistic alterations are most often realized through specification and generalization. As a rule, these operations are accompanied by "quantitative shifts" (Kwieciński 2001: 173), with a visible preference for the condensation. Accordingly, the renditions of lexical elements peculiar to the Polish culture tend to be shorter than in the original. This tendency to amalgamate would seem to have its roots in the translator's assumption that semantically, these lexical items are unnecessary, if not redundant for Polish readers. The compressing operations may be regarded as by-products of shifts in style and semantics, such as generalization, or are implemented in purely quantitative terms by the repackaging/condensation procedure, e.g. by removing the explanatory gloss. The former case is visible in the rendering of "the Poles, Germans, Czechs, Hungarians, Latvians, Lithuanians – all the Eastern and Central Europeans living under communism" (265) as "Polacy, jak i wszystkie inne narody Europy Wschodniej" (217); the latter can be illustrated by the case of "*Tygodnik Powszechny*, the weekly that had published Karol Wojtyla's articles, and Znak, his book publisher, had been shut down" (349) translated as "*Tygodnik Powszechny* i wydawnictwo Znak zostały zamknięte" (279).

From the comparative analysis of the two texts one may infer that if "quantitative shifts" (Kwieciński 2001: 173) overlap with stylistic and semantic alterations, they are inclined to pair as follows: specification/diffusion and generalization/condensation. What is more, it is noteworthy that the former pairing turns out to be a manifestation of the translator's tendency to provide target readers with a much more detailed account of Polish historical figures and events as compared with the source text. The rendition of a short remark concerning Henryk Jabłoński, who was one of the key politicians of the People's Republic of Poland, a long-term head of the Council of State associated with the introduction of the martial law, constitutes a representative example. In the English version Jabłoński is simply referred to as "the president of Poland" (180), while the Polish translation gives the full, official name "Przewodniczący Rady Państwa PRL" (148). This is by no means an isolated case. In a similar manner, the name of one of Edward Gierek's posts within Poland's political system is modified. In the English text Gierek is introduced as "the party chief of Silesia" (123), while in the translation he appears as "szef Komitetu Wojewódzkiego na Górnym Śląsku" (105). Likewise, the reasons for the employment of another frequently encountered translation procedure, covert acculturation, may be assumed to derive from the need for greater specificity. This category of translation procedures can be illustrated by renditions such as "Urząd Bezpieczeństwa" (95) for "Polish secret police" (110), "KC" (300) for "Communist Party headquarters" (379) or "Milicja" (196) for "Police" (238), which are clear representations of domesticating approach. Under this strategy, the translation's fidelity towards the more general perspective shaped from the American vantage point is compromised in order to become plausible and cogent for the Polish readership. Indeed, resting on the fact that the above-mentioned lexical items derive from specifically Polish socio-historical context, such inclination was to be expected.

This, however, is not the case with the subgroup of non-Polish items; yet here, too, the choice of translation procedures seems dictated by a domesticating treatment of the source text. Although culture-specific items from a non-Polish context constitute a minority, their treatment provides a valuable insight into the motivations behind the overall approach employed by the translator. The source text features a few calques and borrowings from languages other than English, particularly Russian. These, however, are not always analogously present in the Polish text and even if they are acknowledged by the translator, their implementation lacks consistency. Such treatment may be exemplified by the treatment of the Russian word "apparatchik", which is rendered differently in two distinctive contexts. When used with reference to an ecclesiastical organ, the word "apparatchik", which evokes a strong emotional (often contemptuous) response, undergoes normalising modification and becomes the rather neutral "aparat" ("aparat Kurii", 147) in the Polish translation. The "curial apparatchik" (180) is therefore deprived of its stereotypical, yet vibrant connotations with corrupt bureaucracy, cynicism, and subservience. On the other hand, when the same expression is employed with regard to the communist system ("communist apparatchik", 123), it is transferred with no semantic alterations as "komunistyczny aparatczyk" (105). Further examples include, to give just a few, "podziemna prasa" (301) as a normalising generalization of "samizdat newspaper" (381), or "polityka wschodnia Papieża" (356) for "the pope's Ostpolitik" (454). As regards the German language, there are only two more occurrences of culture-specific lexical elements in the source text. In the translation they are represented by the borrowed expression "volksdeutscher" (52) and the calqued "cudowny chłopiec" (103) ("wunderkind" in the original). Nonetheless, this group is not devoid of controversial translation operations either, which is due to an extra German element incorporated at the lexical level of the target text. It concerns the description of fierce debates during the Second Vatican Council, which are characterized by viciousness, mutual reluctance and anger. Although the Polish version faithfully preserves the ambience of the Council sessions as depicted in the source text, at one point "sarcastic thrusts" (92) suddenly become "sarkastycznych zwischenrufów" (81), which in this context might suggest a reference to German bishops, although there is no information as to the nationalities of the participants in the original.

When it comes to the sparse Italian and Spanish culture-specific lexical items, the procedure applied involves normalising generalization, accompanied by diffusion. For example, the Argentinian "desaparecidos" (466) in the translation are referred to as "[ci] którzy zaginęli bez śladu" (366) and the phrase "the montoneres guerillas" (458) is rendered as "walka z militarnym reżimem" (365). Finally, it is worth mentioning that when it comes to the transfer of Latin expressions, the translation strategy is open to foreignization. Not only does the translator borrow Latin words at every possible opportunity, but he inserts them even if they are not explicitly present in the English text. The rendition of the titles of the pope's works, when the full Latin title is given instead of or alongside the Polish one, aptly illustrates this tendency. The encyclical "The Splendor of Truth" (132) when mentioned for the first time, is introduced in Polish as "Blask Prawdy" (111) but then, as it reappears throughout the text, it is presented to the target readers as "Veritatis Splendor" (98), in the official language of the Vatican. The nature of such operations is, of course, manifold and should not be regarded as a mere compensation for the avoidance of culture-specific lexical items from other language systems. This matter will be discussed in more detail in the subsequent sections.

Religious lexical items

Even without an in-depth analysis it may be observed that the translated text offers a greater variety of religious expressions. The contrast can be partially attributed to the fact that Polish features two parallel adjectives referring to God ("Boska" and the hypercorrect version "Boża"), and provides various forms of emotionally charged diminutives (e.g. "Najświętsza Panna", "Najświętsza Panienka"), but first and foremost to the translator's deliberate choices, usually oriented towards greater specificity and more pronounced confessional character of the terms. This tendency can be best instantiated by the rendition of the terms "Madonna" and "Black Madonna", which in the Polish version, depending on the context, apart from "Madonna" and "Czarna Madonna" appear as "Święta Panienka", "Najświętsza Panienka", and "Matka Boża Anielska". In the same vein, the object of the pope's fascination changes from "Marian piety" (23) to "tajemnica Wniebowzięcia Najświętszej Maryi" (29), and the icon of the Virgin Mary in the Jasna Góra sanctuary before which JP II prays is "the Mother of Częstochowa" (380) in the original, and "Matka Boska Jasnogórska" (300) in the target text.

Table 1: Confessional diction

the Mother of Częstochowa (108, 124)	1) Matka i Pani Jasnogórska, Matka Boska (95) 2) Matka Boska Częstochowska (101)
Madonna	1) Madonna 2) Czarna Madonna 3) Matka Chrystusowa 4) Matka Boska
Marian piety (23)	Tajemnica Wniebowzięcia Najświętszej Maryi (29)
the Mother of God	1) Matka Boża 2) Matka Boska 3) Maryja 4) Najświętsza Maryja
The Virgin (108)	Święta Dziewica (94)
Shrine of the Holy Virgin (401)	Kościół, kaplica przy sanktuarium Matki Boskiej (315)
Our Lady (23)	Najświętsza Maryja Panna (31)

It might be hypothesized that such specific and varied renditions are partially attributable to the fact that the Polish language system, when compared with the English one, offers more expanded vocabulary referring to Catholic piety. Given the brevity of this paper, an attempt at proving such a hypothesis falls far beyond the scope of the analysis. Nevertheless, the above observations lead to another important issue, which may exert an even greater influence on the divergences in religious lexis, namely the translator's eagerness to improve on the text. The consequences of such translation behaviour may be described in terms of Berman's deforming tendencies.

Portrayal of the pope and the Church

From an analysis of the target text in terms of deforming tendencies it perspires that the predominant and at the same time perhaps the most contentious distortive operations visible in the text are, to some degree interdependent, *ennoblement* and *destruction of underlying networks of signification*.

A conspicuous theme relating to the latter tendency is the avoidance of lexical items referring to sexual issues. This tendency is usually interwoven with qualitative impoverishment and consists in alleviating implications potentially controversial for Polish readers by substituting "sex" with "miłość" (love). For example, in the chapter depicting Wojtyła's teenage years, a reference is made to his friends having "first sexual experiences" (44), while in the translation they appear as "pierwsze doświadczenie miłosne" (44). What is more, any possible sexual connotations are also eschewed, which is well exemplified by the rendition of "they were attracted to each other" (37) as "lubili się" (39). By the same token, Wojtyła's relationship with Anna-Teresa Tymieniecka, a perennial riddle for JP II's biographers, is deprived of its carnal and sensual charge, when her husband's comment "Tymieniecka felt a powerful sexual attraction for the cardinal" (145) is translated as "kardynał pociągał Tymieniecką jako mężczyzna" (120). As seen in the table below, such a treatment is also extended to other persons associated with the Church.

Table 2: Examples of sexuality-related diction removed from the translation

Source text	Target text	Effect of the shift(s)
Karol always went along with her to rehearsals and thought up all sorts of tasks (like waxing her skis) that would leave them together. (36)	Karol przychodził na próby zespołu zawsze z nią, i zawsze mieli mnóstwo tematów do rozmowy, co bardzo ich do siebie zbliżało (38)	no reference to Karol's agency and intention
People didn't like hearing stories about priests who drove around in Mercedes- or were caught by the police roistering at night in the company of half-naked women. (490)	Denerwowały opowieści o księżach, rozpierających się na siedzeniach mercedesów. (585)	reference to sex absent
At audiences, nuns went crazy. They screamed that he was handsomer than Jesus, and they threw themselves at him in hopes of touching him (196)	Tłumy, szczególnie zakonnice, traciły na jego widok głowę. Rozlegały się okrzyki, że jest piękniejszy od Chrystusa. Rzucano się do przodu, byle go tylko dotknąć (162)	impersonal structure (actions no longer explicitly performed by nuns)

As regards ennoblement, in view of the exceptionally high profile John Paul II enjoys in Poland and the idealizing discourse of his compatriots, "rewriting in a more elegant style" (Munday 2001: 150) might have been expected to be a frequently encountered form of "deformation". However, an issue of particular significance is that the translator's manipulative treatment reaches far beyond the stylistic level of the text. One of the translator's regular procedures aimed at the exaltation of John Paul II is omitting troublesome fragments. The scope of deletions performed apparently for the sake of ennoblement extends from the erasure of phrases describing day-to-day, mundane activities and events, such as the pope using a bathroom (see below) or having his tooth knocked out (296), to omissions of his unfavourable opinions concerning Wyszyński and Wałęsa (354 and 350 in the source text, respectively). It is important to note that although the omitted paragraphs are enumerated at the end of the Polish version, deletions of individual phrases and sentences are not acknowledged. An analogous policy is applied to some of the authors' humorous comparisons, disclosing the translator's lack of tolerance towards any departures from the established solemn poetics. A jocular comparison in a sentence describing how the pope "arrived in the city of Gniezno like a modern incarnation of the Spirit, by helicopter" (216) is omitted in the Polish version (179).

Table 3: Portrayal of the pope: examples of reduction of negative features

Source text	Target text	Effect of shift(s)
encouraged by his teachers, tasted the thrill of taking the lead part in school productions (35)	nauczyciele zachęcali go, by wstąpił do gimnazjalnego koła teatralnego (38)	suggesstion of vanity absent
His [Dziwisz's] ability to control Wojtyla's habitual tardiness and his overloaded schedule (266)	umiejętność czuwania nad zawsze przeładowanym programem dnia Wojtyły (235)	reference to tardiness absent
he's a very sophisticated man for somebody who grew up and spent most of his life in Kraków (326)	to bardzo wyrafinowany umysł (261)	belittling qualification absent
a papal commission appointed to consider how to handle the suddenly valuable literary output of Karol Wojtyła (131)	specjalna komisja powołana do zabezpieczenia jego spuścizny literackiej i naukowej (110)	suggestion that the output is not intrinsically valuable absent
He took his meals there, leaving only to visit the chapel or the bathroom. (115)	Nawet jadał samotnie, a schodził jedynie do kaplicy. (99)	mention of bathroom absent
The sexual philosophy of Wojtyla and his flock of Polish Catholics became the rule for the Church universal. (113)	Filozofia Wojtyły w sprawach seksu stała się obowiązującą w całym Kościele. (98)	mention of the 'flock of Polish Catholics' absent

Source text	Target text	Effect of shift(s)
The first papal mass celebrated here seemed almost a coronation in a setting of national religious exaltation. The faithful had massed by the hundreds of thousands in the field outside the walls. (223)	Już pierwsza jego msza w tym miejscu zgromadziła setki tysięcy wiernych. (184)	suggestion of feudal splendor absent
Częstochowa became something like one of the traveling capitals of the medieval emperors. (223)	Częstochowa wydawała się punktem centralnym całej Polski. (184)	suggestion of feudal splendor absent

Within the spiritual dimension, the most striking manifestations of the translator's manipulative treatment of the text include two extreme instances of ennoblement. In the first one, perhaps through an unconscious stylistic shift, the pope seems to be equaled with Jesus Christ: "among the ocean of banners was one proclaiming 'We are with Christ, despite everything'" (222) which in the Polish version appears as "Jedna z grup witała Papieża transparentem, na którym wypisano słowa 'Jesteśmy z Tobą mimo wszystko'" (183). The rendition suggests that in this context the pope is perceived not as a representative, but as an embodiment of God himself. The second occurrence involves a metonymic pattern of using "pope" and "Vatican" interchangeably, as in: "the pope heard nothing of substance for the rest of the day" (340) translated as "aż do końca dnia Watykan nie miał już żadnych informacji" (272).

Again, the ennobling treatment extends to the pope's relationship with the church, and the Catholic church as a whole, as descriptions suggesting discord, excessive wealth, or outdated practices are also toned down, especially where they concern the pope's closest collaborators. For instance, cardinal Dziwisz, who in the source text is presented as a cordial but inquisitive and officious person, on a few occasions is ironically referred to as "don Stanisław", which is ignored in the translation. Interestingly, what is perceived as his shortcomings in the source text, becomes his merits in the Polish version. For example "he was everywhere" (292) is transferred as "jest jego [papieża] prawą ręką" (235), but the most vivid example is the following: "[t]o Italians in the Curia, the most vexing figure in the entourage of the new Polish pope was his chamberlain and private secretary, Monsignor Stanisław Dziwisz" (291), rendered as "[d]la starych wyjadaczy z Kurii Rzymskiej postacią ogromnie drażniącą jest osobisty sekretarz polskiego Papieża, ksiądz Stanisław Dziwisz" (235). Although the notion of conflict is preserved, as if in revenge, "Italians in the Curia" are attributed even more adverse features ("starych wyjadaczy"). Moreover, the deletion of "entourage" and "chamberlain" as well as the substitution of pompous "Monsignor" with the humble "ksiądz" upsets the "surface of iconicity" (Berman in Venuti 2000: 291), which in turn leads to the utterance losing its mocking tenor. On the whole, the above example corroborates the strong interrelations between ennoblement and qualitative impoverishment.

Table 4: Portrayal of the church: examples of reduction of negative features

Source text	Target text	Effect of shift(s)
And afterward the Vatican and the pope behaved rather badly in trying to suppress knowledge of their collaboration. (132)	W późniejszych latach Watykan i Papież nie zachowali się ładnie, usiłując ukryć ten fakt (111)	negation of positive in place of negative; no reference to suppression
On Christmas Eve, as a sign of 'solidarity with suffering nations', the pope lit a candle in the window of his Vatican apartment, a sign that millions of others around the world would soon appropriate. It had been the idea of a Protestant minister in the United States (349)	W wieczór wigilijny, by podkreślić solidarność z cierpiącym narodem, Papież zapalił na oknie swego apartamentu w Watykanie świeczkę. Wiadomość o tym obiegła cały świat i wkrótce w ślad za Ojcem Świętym świeczki takie zapaliły miliony ludzi na całym świecie, katolicy i wyznawcy innych religii. (278)	reference to the Protestant minister absent; 'nations' rendered as 'nation' (suggesting Poland)
The Holy Father wanted to come to Belgium for three days, but the Belgian bishops didn't want him (196)	Ojciec Święty chciał przyjechać do Belgii na dłużej, ale nie stworzono mu po temu warunków (402)	impersonal structure, reference to bishops absent
The harshness of the contest at the ballot box contrasted with the atmosphere of unreal quiet that permeated the conclave (168)	Wszystkim tym rundom głosowań towarzyszyła atmosfera ciszy i głębokiego spokoju (138)	suggestion of internal struggle absent
People were getting tired of the imperial mode with which parish priests publicly demanded their flock pay voluntary tax for the construction or repair of churches. (489/490)	Parafianie byli zmęczeni stylem życia swoich proboszczów, którzy domagali się od nich datków na budowę czy na remonty kościołów. (385)	references to 'flock' and 'imperial mode' absent

Source text	Target text	Effect of shift(s)
From Walters and Casey, the Vatican also received definitive intelligence information – some of it based on intercepted telephone communications – about priests and bishops in Nicaragua and El Salvador (270/271)	Walters i Casey przekazywali również Papieżowi informacje na temat działalności księży w Nikaragui i Salwadorze (221)	no reference to phone tapping
What was new this time, however, was that the people showed little desire to be led, at least by the Church. (489)	Sytuacja była jednak całkiem odmienna niż cztery, osiem i dwanaście lat wcześniej. (385)	no suggestion of dissent

As visible in the above example involving cardinal Dziwisz, deleting uncomfort-
able fragments from the original is not the exclusive means of presenting John
Paul II and his surroundings in a more positive light. The figure of the pope
undergoes exaltation also by means of developing the ideas present in the source
text. For instance "the whole world always has its eyes on the pope" (180), in the
Polish version becomes "przedstawiciele świata mogą obserwować swego ducho-
wego zwierzchnika – papieża" (148). Such glosses are not exactly a compensation
for individual quantitative reductions resulting from deletions, since the general
textual layout is not preserved anyway. The arrangement of paragraphs does not
correspond to that in the source text; moreover, the Polish version is additionally
enriched with photographs of the pope and excerpts from his speeches. Resum-
ing the discussion of ennoblement, it may be observed that removing "unaccep-
table" aspects as well as elaborating on those favourable for the pope constitutes a
discernible pattern of translation behaviour. In some cases the translator goes as
far as transforming what in the original might be considered objections into the
pope's virtues. For instance, "Sometimes he seemed to be choosing in advance
those people who he felt would yield to his charm and rejecting out of hand
those who might not" (116) is translated as "Wielu odnosiło wrażenie, że ma tal-
ent do dobierania sobie ludzi skłonnych ulec sile jego osobowości, zaś odrzuca
pozostałych" (100).

The following example illustrates the translator's readiness to emphasize JP II's
positive features already acknowledged in the source text: "John Paul II pleased the
crowd because he proved a man of flesh and blood, pious but virile. He didn't have
a clerical face" (184) is rendered as "Jan Paweł II od początku swojego pontyfikatu
podbijał serca, gdyż był mężczyzną z krwi i kości. Był pobożnym duchownym, a

jednocześnie miał w sobie tak pociągającą męskość, twarz nie tyle świętego, ile bojownika" (151). Manipulative translation operations identified in the two-sentence excerpt include the introduction of temporal dimension ("od początku swojego pontyfikatu"), which reinforces and validates the ensuing favourable opinion. Secondly, the response to the pontiff is strengthened by the rendition of the rather pejorative "pleased the crowd" as "podbijał serca". The phrase "pious but virile" undergoes clarification, which in turn contributes to expansion. The most striking deviations from the original, however, are the final expressions, where the adjective "clerical" appears as "świętego" (saint), and the expression "twarz (…) bojownika", which might be regarded as a form of semantic mutation, appears without any grounding in the source text; the term used suggests a fighter for a higher cause.

It is worth mentioning that in the light of what has been said in the previous section discussing the translator's attitude towards any traces of sexuality, the above fragment seems to be an exception from the rule. Wojtyła's masculinity is emphasized not only due to the disquisitional rendition of "man" into "mężczyzna", but also through the phrase "podbijać serca", which is not exactly the first phrase that comes to mind in this religious context. Finally, in view of the translator's treatment of sexual issues, "pociągając[a] męskość" with reference to John Paul II sounds potentially scandalous, and might aim at greater plausibility of the figure of John Paul II, which was heretofore dehumanized by the translator's idolising treatment.

Corrections and 'corrections'

One of Berman's most radical assumptions holds that, owing to rationalization and clarification, which together contribute to expansion, the translated text is prone to be of more considerable length than the original. The translated version of Bernstein and Politi's book is indeed longer than its counterpart in the source language, but not only due to the greater average length of Polish lexis or the factors identified by Berman. Starting from the overall layout of the two texts, as already mentioned, it can be observed that the translation changes the arrangement of sentences and paragraphs of the source text. On the whole, the translation is longer not due to the translator's tactic or the idiosyncrasy of the Polish language system, but because it is deliberately "enriched" with additional materials. The quantitative gap resulting from deletions is filled with photographs and fragments of speeches. While the source text includes only individual sentences or paraphrases of John Paul II's literary output, the translation is equipped with whole excerpts from the pope's original speeches and works. What is more, while the pope's individual utterances blend with the text in the original, they are often expanded and given separate sections in the translation.

The translator exhibits a propensity for "correcting" and supplementing the source text. The manifestations of such approach reoccur throughout the translation with a fairly high frequency, in some extreme cases resulting in complete mutations of the source text. The comparative juxtaposition below accurately exemplifies this tendency:

Table 5: Expanded excerpt from the pope's speech

In his homily to another crowd of one million people in the steel town of Katowice (and to the Communist regime), he retreated the basic right of workers: "to a just salary", "to security", "to a day of rest" (380)	W przemówieniu wygłoszonym po mszy w Muchowcu, przed cudownym obrazem Najświętszej Maryi Panny Piekarskiej, Papież do zebranego tu bez mała miliona robotników i pracowników zakładów przemysłowych Śląska mówił o prawach ludzi pracy. "Jest to przede wszystkim prawo do sprawiedliwej zapłaty – sprawiedliwej, czyli takiej, która starczy również na utrzymanie rodziny. Jest to z kolei prawo do zabezpieczenia w razie wypadków związanych z pracą. Jest to również prawo do wypoczynku". (301)

The modifications of the source text involve specifying temporal and spatial dimensions of the pope's speech (from "homily" to "w przemówieniu wygłoszonym po mszy" and from the name of a city to the name of its district, Muchowiec), as well as substituting the authors' paraphrase with an original fragment of the pope's speech.

That the interventions go beyond mere correction of mistakes can be exemplified by the rendition of information concerning cardinal Wyszyński's provenance, which is "peasant class" (99) in the source, and "drobn[a] szlacht[a]" (petty nobility) in the translation (87). The discrepancy does not spring from the lack of a counterpart of "peasant class" on the social ladder in Poland, neither is the change accompanied by any kind of explanation on the side of the translator, for example in the form of a footnote. In fact, even among historians, it turns out it is impossible to reach a general consensus as to cardinal Wyszyński's origin, since, although traditionally he is regarded as noble-born, there is no such entry in the official records. Therefore, the translator's decision to alter this phrase cannot be considered merely as a correction of a factual mistake but should rather be regarded in terms of (literal) ennoblement.

From the readers' perspective, perhaps the most perplexing translational interventions are (apart from 558 references at the end of the Polish version) the footnotes at the bottom of a page. As a rule, such overt glosses refer to the authors' critical remarks concerning the head of the Catholic church, which in the translator's opinion are probably too wrongful or far-fetched and therefore given an immediate rectification; at the same time, they compromise the flow of the text and disturb the process of reading. To give an example, "[w] czasie pobytu w Chile, w kraju znajdującym się pod jarzmem bezwzględnej dyktatury papież nie zdobył się na słowa potępienia przemocy i bezprawia" (365) is "corrected" by the following footnote: "[w] czasie swej wizyty w Chile Jan Paweł II wielokrotnie apelował o odrzucenie wszelkich from przemocy i terroryzmu", followed by comprehensive citations from his speeches. Likewise, an opinion of Ida Magli, a well-known Italian anthropologist, "[j]ego ostre zakazy, w szczególności dotyczące aborcji w każdej sytuacji, noszą pietno nienawisci wobec wolności kobiety" (317) is countered with an additional half-page citation from the pope's "Mulieris dignitatem o godności i powołaniu kobiety", which alleviates the denunciatory tone of the original comment. The translator's interference has also political ramifications, which may be exemplified by the translation of the fragment concerning Andropov's report on the introduction of the state of emergency with a bottom-page footnote reading: "Gen. Wojciech Jaruzelski twierdzi, że w rzeczywistości nigdy nie podpisał takiego dokumentu" (359).

Portrayal of sensitive subjects

As already illustrated, the translator's interventions add up to a more unquestioningly positive image of the pope and the Catholic Church. It is also possible to note three particularly sensitive subjects whose portrayal undergoes shifts: anti-Semitism, Nazism, and Communism.

Analysis of the target text reveals deletions of whole paragraphs addressing the theme of Polish anti-Semitism and the Catholic church's passive consent for the Holocaust, highly debated in contemporary historical as well as socio-political studies. It is worth mentioning that the book was published in Poland in 1997, a decade prior to the publication of *Fear* by Jan Tomasz Gross, which uprooted the cultural typecast of Poles as "Righteous among the Nations", as a consequence of which Gross was sued for offending the Polish nation. Even with a progressive tolerance towards contrary opinions on this issue, it still seems that the majority of Poles are not willing to engage in an open, self-critical discussion devoid of prejudice, let alone in the context of a biography of John Paul II.

Whereas deletions of complete sentences and paragraphs are acknowledged by the translator, there are numerous translation shifts undetectable to a common reader, such as "Studenci organizowali antyniemieckie demonstracje, zdarzały się również wiece antysemickie" (45) translated from "Anti-German demonstrations were commonplace on campus (as were anti-Semitic rallies)" (46), a rendering that plays down the frequency of anti-Semitic demonstrations.

Table 6: *Examples of deletions involving the issue of anti-Semitism*

Source text	Target text	Effect of shift(s)
For the first time ever a Roman pontiff was going to render homage to the victims of the Holocaust, entering the place to which the wartime pope, Pius XIII had closed his eyes. (227)	Po raz pierwszy hołd ofiarom Holocaustu miał oddać Papież. (186)	no reference to Pius XIII
Poland, he thought, was no longer safe for Jews. In Wadowice, young toughs were demanding boycotts of Jewish shops and businesses and smashing their windows. (…) Lieutenant Wojtyla tried to persuade her to stay. "Not all Poles are anti-Semitic. You know I am not!" (44)	–	whole paragraph absent

Continuing the thread of socio-political influences, it is interesting to notice the pattern of rendering "Nazi" (48) as "Niemcy" (46) and "Nazi occupation" (10) as "okupacja hitlerowska" (11), procedures identified as "modification" and "specification" respectively in the analysis of culture-specific lexical items. These operations are not only mild lexical shifts, but deliberate translation choices which have to be approached from a larger, historical perspective. In light of increasingly divergent views on reckoning with the history of World War II, and Germany's collective guilt, the above-mentioned examples seem to reflect the translator's stance on the matter of international contention concerning the distinction between "German" and "Nazi", encouraged in Western countries, but often rejected in Poland.

Although such negligence of "political correctness" might be expected to represent an indication of the translator's global, systematic approach, it is not equally applicable to the also politically charged expression "Soviet". In the Polish language system, there are two equivalents for "Soviet" – the rather pejorative "sowiecki" and, the translator's choice, the more neutral "radziecki". The translator's choice may have been dictated not only by the avoidance of negative associations, but also stylistic reasons. While the translator seems to insist on the collective guilt of Germans, one mention of Soviet liberation of Poland is not likewise "corrected" but eliminated: "The Soviet Union lost six hundred thousand soldiers and officers in the fight to liberate Poland from the Nazis" uttered by a representative of the regime (248) is rendered as "Tam, na tych ziemiach, w latach wojny poległo sześćset tysięcy naszych żołnierzy" (204). In relation to the issue of communism, of special interest is the reduction of occasional comparisons between the policies of communist authorities and those of the pope and the Church.

Table 7: Reduction of comparisons to communist regimes

Source text	Target text	Effect of shift(s)
It's certainly a paradox of history that this great anti-Communist warrior should use language so similar to that of the Communist leaders who for decades used to warn the peoples of Eastern Europe and the Soviet Union against contamination by the "decadent" West. (496)	–	whole paragraph omitted
They lobbied the media to promote "Christian values" (just as the Communist Party had once demanded that the media conform to Marxist-Leninist principles) (490)	Kler chciał czegoś w rodzaju cenzury programów telewizyjnych. Zabiegał o wprowadzenie ustawy, nakazującej przestrzegania w telewizji „wartości chrześcijańskich" (385)	no comparison to communism

Conclusion

His Holiness may be regarded as an extreme manifestation of a translation approach which succumbs to the idolising dicursive mode, or what in Lefevere's terminology would be termed dominant poetics, of portraying the Polish pope. Within a non-textual dimension, the motivations behind translation decisions may both be attributed to patronage or constraints imposed on the translator by a clear-cut ideological framework.

As regards specific translation operations, the analysis resting on Kwieciński's consolidated taxonomy as its theoretical point of reference revealed that the overall bias may be placed within the borderlines of normalization in the case of culture specific lexical items re-embedded into the domestic context, and closer

towards intense domestication as regards those from outside the cultural framework of Poland. In terms of Berman's deforming tendencies, predominantly encountered translation shifts include qualitative impoverishment, the destruction
of underlying networks of signification and ennoblement, appearing individually or, due to their interdependent nature, most often in clusters. The rendition
of religious vocabulary disclosed the translator's predilection to more detailed
expressions denoting religious figures and objects of worship. An issue of particular importance is that, regardless of the methodology applied, the study revealed miscellaneous translation operations aimed at exalting the figure of the
Polish pontiff and alleviating or simply eschewing any criticism of him.

One of the most significant by-products of such detrimental treatment of the
original is that it becomes deprived of its unique "subtext" (Berman in Venuti
2000: 292), which is exactly what distinguishes Bernstein and Politi's book and
makes it an appreciated and internationally recognizable biography. A considerable majority of "troublesome" fragments, involving the authors' direct allega-
tions or meant to be read between the lines, are consistently mitigated. Direct
ramifications of subscribing the foreign text into an idolising discursive mode
contribute to the overall impression that the translation is devoid of the original's characteristic, slightly ironic, discursive tone. Apart from conforming to the
dominant poetics, the translator's apparent determination to improve the source
text was also identified and illustrated in the study. This mechanism is closely
tied with what in Kwieciński's terminology would be referred to as normaliza-
tion/specification procedure, but also differs in the sense that it usually involves
deliberate translation choices to correct what the translator thought a mistake or
inaccuracy in the original.

The question remains why, despite all the trouble necessary to adjust it to the
target literary canon, the publishers chose the text at all. Resting on Even-Zohar's
theoretical framework, it can be observed that, at the micro-level of the Polish
literary polysystem, domestic literature on John Paul II assumes the central sphere
within the system of religious literature. The publisher's choice for the text to be
translated seems to be motivated by economic factors, and the desire to capitalize
on the international prestige enjoyed by Politi, a famous Vaticanist and journalist
of leading Italian dailies, and Bernstein, a Pulitzer Prize-winner world-famous for
work that is the very opposite of uncontroversial laudatory journalism.

References

Berman, Antoine. 2000. "Translation and the trials of the foreign", in Venuti,
    Lawrence (ed.) *The translation studies reader*, 285–297.

Bernstein, Carl and Marco Politi. 1996. *His Holiness. John Paul II and the hidden history of our times*. New York: Doubleday.

Bernstein, Carl and Marco Politi. 1997. *Jego Świątobliwość. Jan Paweł II i ukryta historia naszych czasów*. Warszawa: Wydawnictwo Amber.

Even-Zohar, Itamar. 2000. "The position of translated literature within the literary polysystem", in Lawrence Venuti (ed.) *The translation studies reader*, 192–197.

Hatim, Basil and Jeremy Munday. 2004. *Translation. An advanced resource book*. London and New York: Routledge.

Hatim, Basil and Ian Mason. 1997. *The translator as communicator*. London and New York: Routledge.

Kwieciński, Piotr. 2001. *Disturbing strangeness. Foreignization and domestication in translation procedures in the context of cultural asymmetry*. Toruń: Wydawnictwo EDYTOR.

Lefevere, Andre (ed.) 1992a. *Translation / History / Culture. A sourcebook*. London and New York: Routledge.

Lefevere, Andre. 1992b. *Translation, rewriting and the manipulation of literary frame*. London and New York: Routledge.

Munday, Jeremy. 2008. *Introducing translation studies*. London and New York: Routledge.

Sikorski, Radek. 2005. "The Pope as Pole", *National Review* 57. 7, 40–41.

Toury, Gideon. 1995. *Descriptive Translation Studies and beyond*. Amsterdam/ Philadelphia: John Benjamins.

Toury, Gideon. 2000. "The nature and role of norms in translation", in Lawrence Venuti (ed.) *The translation studies reader*, 198–211.

Venuti, Lawrence. 1995. *The translator's invisibility. A history of translation*. London and New York: Routledge.

Venuti, Lawrence. 1998. *The scandals of translation. Towards an ethics of difference*. London and New York: Routledge.

Ewa Tadajewska

Domestication and foreignization in children's literature. Culture-specific items in two Polish translations of *Anne of Green Gables*

The role of translators as mediators is strongly felt in children's literature, because it is among others through translations that monolingual children get to know foreign cultures. Mediation does not have to be neutral (Van Coillie and Verschueren 2006: v); as Van Coillie and Verschueren state,

> translators do not simply stand 'in between' source text and target audience, from the beginning they are always an intrinsic part of negotiating dialogue itself, holding a fragile, unstable middle between the social forces that act upon them (the imposed norms of the publishing industries and the expectations of the adults who act as buyers and often as co-readers), their own interpretation of the source text and their assessment of the target audience […]. (Van Coillie and Verschueren 2006: v)

What is more, translators are mediators of more than cultural and social context but also the values and expectations of childhood which are encoded in the original text (Lathey 2010: 196). In short, a translator shapes the image of the text which readers are to receive. Therefore, translation of children's books is a complex literary challenge (Van Coillie and Verschueren 2006: v), especially when there are pronounced differences between source and target culture.

Such mediation is visible in the Polish translations of *Anne of Green Gables*, one of the most popular English-Canadian novels, with respect to religious issues. The book has been a bestseller since its first publication in 1908, a "Canadian classic" whose protagonist, Anne Shirley, is regarded a "national icon", a "symbol of Canadianness" and Canada's main "commodity export" (Devereux 2001: 11). Despite cultural specificity, as well as political and ideological implications, *Anne of Green Gables* is considered universal. As Cecily Devereux states, "its representations of childhood, girlhood, family life and communities have been understood as essential, eternal and natural" (20). Mark Twain described Anne as "the dearest and most lovable child in fiction since the immortal Alice" (Twain in Brennan 1995: 248).

Translated into many languages, the novel has attracted both young and adult readers. Its first Polish translation was published in 1912. (Rubio and Waterston 1995: 123). The novel was then retranslated several times.

Retranslation of children's literature

The retranslation of children's books is "a multifunctional aspect of the publishing industry" (Lathey 2010: 174). It concerns mostly those texts which are considered 'classics' (174). In most cases, the publication of a fresh translation does not necessarily mean that the old one is not read; the reasons for retranslation are usually utterly different (161).

Lathey states that "[i]n the long history of the retranslation of texts for children, the impetus for new versions may be educational, literary, commercial, or a combination of the three" (161). In some cases, translators are dissatisfied with old versions and they encourage publishers to produce a new edition of a given book. The initiative may also come from editors claiming that the existing version is unsuitable for children in terms of language and tone, or noticing the growing interest in scholarly editions of children's classics. However, usually the most common commercial reasons are re-edition or repackaging of a book and the publication of an anniversary edition. There are many cases when a great illustrator is the "catalyst" for retranslation. (161)

The retranslation of children's books after a long period "involves a reconsideration of an implied reader" (162). Usually, if classics are used for scholarly purposes, references to history are preserved. However, according to Lathey, there are also instances when the opposite process occurs: "domestication of historical detail and linguistic modernisation [which] transforms an antiquated translation into a child-friendly edition for contemporary young readers" (162).

Another aspect of retranslation is the decision whether to take the existing versions into consideration. There are translators who only read the old editions after the completion of their work, because they do not want to be influenced. Others study existing versions and use them to compare and improve their efforts. (2010: 161) Sometimes in retranslations of popular books, readers can notice new aspects. Such is the case of the depiction of cultural and religious issues in the 1912 and 2003 Polish translations of *Anne of Green Gables*.

Lucy Maud Montgomery and Presbyterianism

Lucy Maud Montgomery's family history locates her within the context of Scottish Presbyterian culture. Her cultural impact is an essential part of the heritage of Scottish community in Canada. The impact is rooted "in the religious and cultural ethos of the Scottish-Canadian society in which she was raised" (Rubio 1999: 89), a continuation of her ancestors' views on religion, education, egalitarianism and other important issues.

Montgomery grew up on Prince Edward Island, in "an enclave of Scots" who were very proud of their cultural heritage. Her ancestors had been in the first wave of emigrants who decided to come to Prince Edward Island. According to Mary Henley Rubio, "their clannishness, the moral seriousness, their Presbyterian belief in Protestant work ethic, their faith in the possibility of human improvement, and their insistence on setting up the best possible school systems for all the children without prejudice of social class – all this contributed to their success and their subsequent pride in this success" (90).

Scottish immigrants brought to Canada their beliefs and principles, which emphasized self-examination, valuing intellect and achievement, 'plain speaking' and participatory democracy in the church (89). They held that education should be accessible to all people, including women. Therefore, Montgomery attended good schools, and later she took a firm stand for women's education in her writing (92).

From the Scottish heritage Montgomery also retained a conviction that telling stories was a good way to change public attitudes. For Scottish Presbyterians the Bible was not only "a source for theological points to argue about" (92), but also a book containing "stories and examples of teaching through stories and parables" (92). In Cavendish, where Montgomery grew up, Presbyterians read the Bible every day. In consequence, as Rubio claims, "Montgomery's fiction draws on the storytelling of her cultural milieu, too, as well as on the general ethos of Presbyterianism" (92).

Moreover, social heritage of Presbyterianism is reflected in Montgomery's representation of the community which examines itself. Presbyterians were taught by their religion "to constantly examine their own lives for signs of slackness" (93). They tended to be strict for themselves and often extended this 'controlling process' to their relatives and neighbors. According to Rubio, "Montgomery's stories are laced with judgments about people's morality, theology, behaviour, and general rectitude. This constant judging of others is a religious exercise in the purest sense, for it shows up the people who are mean-spirited, selfish, and otherwise unworthy of God's grace" (93). In her novels, there are always characters who talk about other people's faults and imperfections and treat it as their Christian duty. They justify their 'plain speaking' by the view that humility is necessary to get into Heaven. (93)

There is also another factor which could influence Montgomery's writing. In 1903, Reverend Ewan Macdonald, a new minister, was inducted into the Cavendish church (Rubio and Waterston 1995: 123). Montgomery, as a church organist, met him regularly (40). They became engaged in 1906, and it was during the period of engagement that she wrote her first novel, *Anne of Green Gables* (123).

Religion in *Anne of Green Gables* as a culture-specific field

The protagonist of the book, Anne Shirley, arrives at Green Gables and starts her life in a conservative society, similar to that surrounding Montgomery, where religion is at the centre of daily life (Brennan 1995: 251). People attend masses and prayer-meetings, children go to Sunday school, and Mrs Rachel Lynde comments on whether her neighbours live according to Christian faith.

Anne's 'religious education' is shown with humor. During her first visit to a Presbyterian church, she spends time looking out of the window and dreaming. As Rubio explains, "Montgomery is undoubtedly reflecting some of her childhood feelings of being cooped up in a church when she might have been out running through the fields and playing. She also is touching on a theme that comes up repeatedly in her novels: long prayers and tedious sermons that a captive child – and indeed captive adults – must endure" (Rubio 1999: 95). Apparently, the writer sympathized with Anne's idea of prayer, which consisted of going to the forest and looking up into the sky (Brennan 1995: 253). Nevertheless, despite the protagonist's departures from orthodoxy, in Montgomery's fiction, Presbyterian faith becomes an important part of her characters' identity.

Given the significance of religion for Montgomery and her community, it is not surprising that in *Anne of Green Gables* readers can find names of prayers, religious texts, church organizationsand many other cultural terms.

Cultural items in the 1912 and the 2003 Polish translations of *Anne of Green Gables*

The present case study consists in an analysis of the first Polish translation of Lucy Maud Montgomery's book *Anne of Green Gables*, done by Rozalia Bernsteinowa in 1912, and Agnieszka Kuc's translation, which was published in 2003. This comparison is concerned with procedures for the translation of religious terms, such as names of prayers, religious writings, festivals and church organizations. They will be discussed in accordance with the terminology developed by Piotr Kwieciński in *Disturbing Strangeness*. Kwieciński provides a consolidated classification of procedures for the translation of culture-specific items. They can be divided into four general groupings: exoticising procedures, including borrowing and calque; rich explicatory procedures, such as borrowing + calque, borrowing or calque + normalization (gloss); assimilative procedures, encompassing recognized exoticism, normalization, deletion, covert or overt cultural substitution; and other combinations, such as couplets, triplets and quadruplets. (Kwieciński 2001: 157–161)

Faced with foreign lexical items, translators may use ad hoc and recent *borrowing*. The former one can be called importation. The latter relates to those words which are not fully absorbed in the target culture. The most common distancing devices are inverted commas or qualifiers. Another procedure is *calque*, grouped with coinage and semantic extension. In general, it is a "through-translation" of a word from the source language to the target language (158). In many cases calques are linguistically disruptive (162). Translators may combine procedures in various ways. Those combinations which include normalised *gloss* can be subdivided according to its type. Extratextual gloss is an "exoticising visible intervention of the translator" (162–163, such as the use of footnotes; by contrast, intratextual gloss is an embedded gloss, which blends with the text (163). The next procedure is *recognized exoticism*, which consists in using "recognized equivalents" for source culture-specific elements which are considered foreign concepts by the target culture, but are intelligible (163). *Normalization* is "rendering a SC [source culture]-specific items in supposedly 'transcultural' terms" (163). Its subcategories are: generic normalization, repackaging, generalization, specification, modification and mutation (159). Another procedure, *deletion*, is simply an omission of a source culture-specific element in translation (163). *Covert cultural substitution* is the replacement of a source culture-specific element with a target culture-specific element. It does not appear to the recipients as translation manipulation, whereas *acculturation* consists in "introducing a TC-specific item where the SL version offers a more generalised transcultural content" (164). Finally, *overt cultural substitution* is the replacement of a source culture-specific word with a target culture-specific which does not exist in the source culture (164). *Overt acculturation* is very similar, but it introduces a "manifestly TC-specific item where the source text has a transcultural item" (165). The use of the procedures described above will be analysed on the example of two Polish translations of *Anne of Green Gables*.

Case study

When Anne Shirley arrives in Green Gables, her religious education begins. As she is taught how to pray, such prayers as "Now I lay me down to sleep" and the Lord's Prayer are mentioned.

Table 1: Prayers

Montgomery	Bernsteinowa	Strategy	Kuc	Strategy
"Now I lay me down to sleep"	„Kiedy się do snu układam"	calque	„Aniele Boży"	covert cultural substitution
The Lord's Prayer	„Ojcze nasz"	covert cultural substitution	„Modlitwa Pańska"	calque

In the first Polish translation, names of prayers are translated by using calques, which are exoticizing procedures, or by applying covert cultural substitution, an assimilative method. Both translations of the Lord's Prayer are comprehensible, but those of "Now I lay me down to sleep" cause problems. "Kiedy się do snu układam" is unknown for Polish readers while "Aniele Boży", a recognized Catholic prayer, obscures the foreign element.

Many religious terms appear in the book when Anne starts to attend Sunday school, where reading the Bible and other appropriate religious writings is an indispensable element of education.

Table 2: Religious education

Montgomery	Bernsteinowa	Strategy	Kuc	Strategy
Sunday school	szkoła niedzielna	calque	szkółka niedzielna	recognized exoticism
testament reading	lekcja religii	covert cultural substitution	studiowanie Biblii	calque
the Peep of Day series	modlitewnik dla młodzieży	normalization, generalization	odpowiednie rzeczy do czytania	normalization, mutation

As can be seen from Table 2, within this category, in both analyzed translations various strategies were used. However, in general, assimilative procedures prevail.

The next group of culture-specific items is related to the most important institution in Presbyterian life – the church, as Anne Shirley and other characters, including Marilla and Mrs Lynde, take part in the church life.

Table 3: Church

Montgomery	Bernsteinowa	Strategy	Kuc	Strategy
minister	pastor	recognised exoticism	pastor	recognized exoticism
ministers	księża	covert cultural substitution	pastorzy	recognized exoticism
ministers	pastorowie	recognised exoticism	duchowni	normalization
prayer-meeting	zebranie	normalization	nabożeństwo	normalization, generalization
manse	plebania	covert cultural substitution	Plebania	covert cultural substitution

In both translations, there is no consistency concerning the term *ministers*. It is translated into various words, which can be confusing for readers. However, in general, within this category, assimilative procedures prevail. The only exception is recognized exoticism, which according to Kwieciński is a borderline case between exoticization and assimilation (Kwieciński 2001: 163).

Being active in the church life involves membership in religious organizations, whose names constitute the next group of items.

Table 4: Organizations

Montgomery	Bernsteinowa	Strategy	Kuc	Strategy
the Aids	panie ze związku	normalization, generalization	panie z kółka charytatywnego	normalization
Aid's meeting	posiedzenie związku	normalization, generalization	zebrania parafialne	normalization, modification
Church Aid Society	parafialny Związek Pomocy	calque	parafialny oddział koła pomocy	calque
Foreign Missions Auxiliary	Stowarzyszenie Pomocy dla Misjonarzy nawracających dalekich pogan	calque + internal gloss	Stowarzyszenie Misyjne	partial calque
the Red Crosses	–	deletion	Czerwony Krzyż	recognized exoticism
the White Sands Baptist Choir	Białe Piaski	calque + deletion	miejscowy chór kościoła baptystów	normalization + internal gloss + calque

As can be seen from the above table, Kuc, similarly to Bersteinowa, uses combinations of strategies. What is more, in both translations there appear explicatory procedures, namely combinations of calques and internal glosses.

Since Montgomery's book describes a long period of time in the girl's life, conversations about such ceremonies as weddings are an obvious element of the novel. Furthermore, celebrating festivals, which is an indispensable part of childhood, is also depicted; for instance, Chapter 25, "Matthew insists on Puffed Sleeves", is concerned with Christmas.

Table 5: Religious festivals and ceremonies

Montgomery	Bernsteinowa	Strategy	Kuc	Strategy
Christmas	Gwiazdka	overt cultural substitution	święta	calque
Christmas morning	poranek wigilijny	covert cultural substitution	rano w dzień Bożego Narodzenia	calque
nobody ever has been married in the church yet	obecnie bierze się już tylko śluby cywilne	covert cultural substitution	nikt jeszcze nie brał ślubu w kościele + gloss Kościół prezbiteriański uznaje tylko dwa sakramenty: chrzest i komunię. Małżeństwo nie jest sakramentem.	calque + external gloss
wedding	wesele	calque	ślub w kościele	calque + internal gloss

The above examples indicate a significant difference between the 1912 and the 2003 translations. In the former one, mostly assimilative procedures are applied, particularly cultural substitution. For instance, Bernsteinowa's translation of "Christmas morning" may result in confusion, since the target term refers to 25 December, not to 24 December, i.e. Christmas Eve. Children living in Poland can be surprised by the fact that Anne gets a present in the morning on Christmas Eve; the translator apparently domesticates the date connected with presents while leaving the time of day unchanged. In contrast to this rendering, Kuc chooses exoticization. All examples from her version presented in Table 5 are calques, in two instances supplemented by a gloss.

Finally, the wide range of terms which are connected with religion includes such items as names of people and book titles.

Table 6: Other items

Montgomery	Bernsteinowa	Strategy	Kuc	Strategy
paraphrase	przypowieści	normalization, mutation	pieśni i hymny	normalization
nineteenth paraphrase	19 przypowieść	normalization, mutation	pieśń 19	normalization
the fathers and mothers in Israel	„ojcowie i matki gminy"	calque + normalization	członkowie wspólnoty parafialnej	normalization
Moody Spurgeon	Moody Spurgeon + gloss Moody i Spurgeon to nazwiska dwóch najpopularniejszych kaznodziejów w Ameryce	borrowing + external gloss	Moody Spurgeon + gloss Dwight Lyman Moody (1837–1899) – słynny amerykański kaznodzieja, w 1889 r. utworzył Instytut Biblijny w Chicago. Charles Haddon Spurgeon (1834–1892) – wybitny angielski kaznodzieja Kościoła baptystów, który uzyskał przydomek „Książę kaznodziejów".	borrowing + external gloss
Ben-Hur	"Ben Hur"	borrowing	Ben Hur + gloss powieść historyczna Lewisa Wallace'a (1827–1905), opublikowana w 1880. Opowiada o początkach chrześcijaństwa.	borrowing + external gloss

There is a significant difference concerning the translation of the word "para-phrase". Although both translations used normalization, in the 1912 version this term is translated as *przypowieść* (parable), and in the 2003 version as *pieśń* (song). Kuc explains her choice by stating that in Bernsteinowa's translation the term *przypowieść* is preceded by the number, which can confuse the readers (Kuc 2008: 4), as parables are not numbered.

The example regarding Moody Spurgeon requires information about con-text. In *Anne of Green Gables*, Moody Spurgeon MacPherson is the protagonist's friend. When Anne says: "Moody Spurgeon is going to be a minister. Mrs Lynde says he couldn't be anything else with a name like that to live up" (Montgomery 2008 [1908]: 300), Bernsteinowa and Kuc explain the allusion in a gloss.

Conclusions

The present case study shows that in both analyzed translations of Lucy Maud Montgomery's *Anne of Green Gables* assimilative procedures prevail. The most common strategies are cultural substitution, recognized exoticism and normaliza-tion. Cultural substitution and deletion are especially common in Bernsteinowa's version, while glosses are more common and more extensive in the translation by Kuc. Only in a few examples calque and borrowings appear in the target text.

Several translated terms may cause problems in the text's comprehension. For instance, Kuc points out that readers of the first Polish translation may initially have problems with specifying Anne's denomination (Kuc 2008: 4), due to the fact that the word *ministers* was translated into *księża*, a term connected with Catholicism, not Protestantism.

Taking everything into account, exoticization is still a rarer method. To use Venuti's terminology, domestication is applied more often than foreignization, and both translations to some extent convert Protestant terms into Catholic ones. However, in the later translation foreignizing procedures are more frequent than in Bernsteinowa's version.

References

Brennan, Joseph Gerard. 1995. "The story of a classic: Anne and after", *American Scholar* 64.2, 247–256.

Devereux, Cecily. 2001. "'Canadian classic' and 'commodity export': The nation-alism of 'our' *Anne of Green Gables*", *Journal of Canadian studies* 36.1, 11–28.

Gammel, Irene and Elizabeth Epperly (eds.) 1999. *L.M. Montgomery and Cana-dian culture*. Toronto: University of Toronto Press.

Kuc, Agnieszka. "*Ania z Zielonego Wzgórza* w nowym tłumaczeniu", ania. wydawnictwoliterackie.pl/konferencja_metodyczna_krakow_2008.pdf, DOA January 7, 2011.

Kwieciński, Piotr. 2001. *Disturbing strangeness: foreignisation and domestication in translation procedures in the context of cultural asymmetry*. Toruń: EDYTOR.

Lathey, Gillian. 2010. *The role of translators in children's literature: Invisible storytellers*. New York: Routledge.

Montgomery, Lucy Maud. 2001. *Ania z Zielonego Wzgórza*, trans. R. Bernsteinowa. Warszawa: Prószyński i S-ka.

Montgomery, Lucy Maud. 2003. *Ania z Zielonego Wzgórza*, trans. A. Kuc. Kraków: Wydawnictwo Literackie.

Montgomery, Lucy Maud. 2008. *Anne of Green Gables*. London: Puffin.

Rubio, Mary and Elizabeth Waterston. 1995. *Writing a life: L.M. Montgomery*. Toronto: ECW Press.

Rubio, Mary Henley. 1999. "L.M. Montgomery: Scottish-Presbyterian Agency in Canadian Culture", in Irene Gammel and Elizabeth Epperly (eds.) *L.M. Montgomery and Canadian culture*, 89–105.

Van Coillie, Jan and Walter P. Verschueren (eds.) 2006. *Children's literature in translation: Challenges and strategies*. Manchester: St. Jerome Publishing.

Van Coillie, Jan and Walter P. Verschueren. 2006. "Editor's Preface", in Jan Van Coillie and Walter P. Verschueren (eds.) *Children's literature in translation: Challenges and strategies*, v–ix.

Venuti, Lawrence. 1995. *The translator's invisibility: History of translation*. London and New York: Routledge.

Polish to English:
the exotic East

Karolina Retkowska

Old Polish attire in English. Foreignness and domesticity in the English translations of Adam Mickiewicz's *Pan Tadeusz*

Adam Mickiewicz's *Pan Tadeusz* is regarded a literary codification of contemporaneous Polishness as it constitutes an unsurpassed illustration of Polish life in the nineteenth century, depicting the lifestyle, customs and traditions of those times. Mickiewicz was able to realistically encapsulate the characteristic features of Polish life and create an immortal monument of the Polish spirit at the end of the culture of nobility (Chlebowski 1917: 117).

Pan Tadeusz, being the Polish national epic, is perhaps the most important book for the Polish nation. Taking into consideration its huge impact on the national consciousness of Poles, as well as the fact that it is one of the most outstanding and unique works in Polish, its translator faces one of the greatest possible difficulties in translation. Aleksader Wit Labuda, in his article on the French translation series of *Pan Tadeusz*, stated that "in the case of *Pan Tadeusz* there are so many problems that a person who undertakes its translation may entrust their soul only to Sisyphus' care" (Labuda 1993: 67; trans. Karolina Retkowska). All the more astonishing is the fact that as many as seven translators have taken up the challenge to translate the epic into English.

The aim of this paper is to establish to what extent foreignizing strategies have been used to stress the cultural uniqueness of a text that has attained the status of a national symbol, on the example of one element only: traditional Polish attire.

Historical and cultural background

After the Third Partition (1795), the Polish-Lithuanian Commonwealth disappeared from the map of Europe. Although the occupying powers used all possible denationalization measures, prohibiting Polish language, persecuting religion and destroying institutions, Poland did not perish as it survived in the minds of its inhabitants (Miłosz 1969: 195). The nobility culture became a bastion of Polishness and a nobleman became an icon of the old Pole: a reveler and often a brawler, but a free person who was victorious in battles against the invaders (Tazbir 1978: 177–178).

Polish people saw hope of restoring the Polish state in Napoleon. In 1797, the Polish Napoleonic legion was created in Italy and after several years the Napoleonic army triumphed over Prussia, which led to the creation of the Duchy of Warsaw in 1807. Thereafter, in 1812, troops of the Duchy participated in the invasion of Russia, which ended in Napoleon's defeat. Nevertheless, the Congress in Vienna created a new Polish state, the "Congress Kingdom", whose nominal head was the Russian Tsar. In the 1820s, a romantic revolutionary movement spread through Poland as the Tsar did not respect the Constitution of 1815. In November 1830 an uprising broke out and amounted to a war with Russia. Russia's victory resulted in Great Emigration: thousands of officers, soldiers and intellectuals migrated mainly to France. After the uprising, the Kingdom of Poland was preserved, but it was weak and brutally repressed. (Miłosz 1969: 195–198) Paris became the headquarters of the Polish government in exile and the centre of Polish culture abroad. The atmosphere in the émigré community was very tense as emigrants were deeply involved in political quarrels and intrigues (Debska 2000: 102). In such circumstances, between 1832 and 1834, Adam Mickiewicz created one of the most outstanding works in Polish literature – Pan Tadeusz. The poet himself stated in his Epilogue to Pan Tadeusz that in the alien environment of exile he felt like an uninvited guest:

> For us unbidden guests in every clime
> From the beginning to the end of time
> There is but one place in the planet whole
> Where happiness may be for every Pole –
> The land of childhood! that shall aye endure
> As holy as a first love and pure (Mickiewicz 2009 [1834]: 582)[1]

In his new undertaking, he found an "island to which he could escape, closing the door on Europe's noises" (Miłosz 1969: 227). Pan Tadeusz has very little to do with the ideological conflicts of the day since Mickiewicz decided that the severely hurt Polish nation needed to look for solace in the carefree childhood days. The poet intended to create a plain rural idyll in the style of Goethe's Hermann und Dorothea. However, the poem expanded to a masterpiece divided into twelve books, composed of almost ten thousand verses of Polish alexandrine (thirteen syllable feminine rhyming couplets with caesura after the seventh syllable). (Miłosz 1969: 227)

The story of Pan Tadeusz is set in the fictitious country estate of Soplicowo in Lithuania, over the course of five days in 1811 and one day in 1812, the years

---

1   translated by Kenneth R. Mackenzie.

preceding Napoleon's war on Russia. At that time, Polish nobility awaited him, hoping that the war would bring the restoration of Polish statehood. Gentry patriotism, fondness of the Polish culture and attachment to tradition preserved old customs intact for a very long time. The cultivation of traditions in Soplicowo is reflected in the utterance of Bartek, one of the characters of the poem:

> Whene'er I come back from some Prussian place
> And long to wash away all German trace,
> I run to Soplicowo, heart of Poland, where
> A man may drink his country with the air! (Mickiewicz 2009 [1834]: 318)[2]

With a mission of providing a specimen of pure Polish life, the poem has shaped the national consciousness of Poles for years and has become the object of numerous literary references, as well as the subject of endless associations, reflections, allusions and paraphrases (Teodorowicz-Hellman 2006: 349). Professor George Rapall Noyes in the introduction to his translation of *Pan Tadeusz* explains the significance of this poem to Polish people:

> Perhaps no other poem of any other European nation is so truly national and in the best sense of the word popular. Almost every Pole who has read anything more than the newspaper is familiar with the content of Pan Tadeusz. No play of Shakespeare, no long poem of Milton or Wordsworth or Tennyson, is so well known or so well beloved by the English people as is Pan Tadeusz by the Poles. To find a work equally well known one might turn to Defoe's prosaic tale of adventure, Robinson Crusoe; to find a work so beloved would be hardly possible. (Noyes, in Mickiewicz 1917 [1834]: x)

According to Bronisław Chlebowski (in Skibińska 2006: 253), the representation of nobility customs in *Pan Tadeusz* is so full and faithful that the poem has become not only a great masterpiece of poetry but also a document of the internal history of Polish nation, depicting an idealized vision of a lifestyle that

> had already gone or was just disappearing, or perhaps never existed in this particular form. It does not matter. It exists and will continue to form our ideas about authentically Polish life, native customs and landscapes, in which a truly happy life goes on. Hence Mickiewicz's Pompeii – Soplicowo, in a way a synthetic image of Polishness, is an essence of everything one would like to protect from annihilation, (...) stored in memory and recorded in sentiments as important, characteristic, distinctive, good and beloved. (Witkowska, in Skibińska 2006: 266; trans. Karolina Retkowska)

Therefore, translators of *Pan Tadeusz* should strive to protect the unique culture of the Polish nobility era and be aware of the cultural ramifications of their choices.

---

2   translated by Kenneth R. Mackenzie.

Elements of traditional Polish attire as
an important cultural aspect

The history of Polish attire has been recently evoking more and more interest. It is no longer treated only as some curiosity of the past, since historians have begun to strive for an integral apprehension of history, and thus full reproduction of people's lifestyles, their needs, aspirations and values (Bartkiewicz 1979: 7). The nobility culture shaped the image of the Polish nobleman as a descendant of mythologized Sarmatian warriors, which was very important in self-determination of the nobility and in emphasizing their separateness from other social strata. Clothing is one of the elements that very strongly defines the specificity of Polish nobility's customs. It is worth mentioning that many items of clothing comprising the traditional Old Polish costume are of Turkish origin. According to Gloger (1978, vol. III: 79), *kontusz* became the dominant costume of the Polish nobility as a result of victorious battles against the Turks. Poles, as proud winners, treated the Turkish *kontusz* as a trophy and wore it on the Polish *żupan*. Therefore, this costume brings back memories of a heroic past.

Janusz Tazbir (1978: 41) points out that during the nobility era in Poland, one's outfit was not only a personal manifestation of fashion, and it revealed not only marital status, age or occupation, but, above all, one's social position, as well as political views. Politically, garments expressed either an oppositional or a loyal stance. A gentleman wearing *żupan* and *kontusz* was regarded as a supporter of the so called "golden freedom" of noble democracy. By contrast, a person dressed in a French costume provoked suspicions that they intend to overthrow the institution of free election and impose absolutism (Tazbir 1978, 41–42). Bartkiewicz (1979: 109) claims that during the period of Partitions, a conscious popularization of traditional Polish attire was initiated, so that Polish dress grew into a symbol of patriotism and all civic virtues. Furthermore, Bartkiewicz states that in no previous era was attire so important, nor was its distinctiveness stressed more audaciously as a manifestation of national identity. According to Tazbir (1978: 42), the partitioning powers, especially Russia, knew exactly what they were doing when they prohibited the wearing of *kontusz* or *czamara*. Therefore, patriots wore national attire, while those with cosmopolitan beliefs (especially magnates) adhered to foreign costumes.

As a result, numerous patriotic poets often openly criticized the European fashion and promoted the national dress code. *Pamiętnik Warszawski*, published in 1819, featured a patriotic poem which Bartkiewicz attributes to Kazimierz Brodziński:

Wear kontuszes, noble brotherhood!
For if you want to be a perfect Pole
It's not enough to have a Polish soul
You need to shed the tailcoat for good.[3] (in Bartkiewicz 1979: 127; trans. Karolina Retkowska)

Tazbir (1978: 42) mentions an anonymous poet who reckoned that together with the national attire, Polish language can perish. Yet another anonymous author in *Pszczoła Polska* in 1820 called for abandoning foreign fashion, coquetry and snobbery, and instead returning to the customs of ancestors (Bartkiewicz 1979: 127). This author believed that the contemporaneous popularization of traditional Polish attire could be the starting point for the revival of Old Polish virtues, and, as a consequence, for the resurrection of traditional lifestyle, and maybe even state.

In *Pan Tadeusz* all the features of traditional lifestyle, from the *karabela* and the scapular, to Polish cuisine and national dances, compose the moral and ideological model of the Polish gentry culture and its struggle against Russians (Tazbir 1978: 188). According to Borejszo (2008: 240), fashion in *Pan Tadeusz* constitutes a vital part of the image of Polish-Lithuanian Commonwealth of the early nineteenth century. Krupianka (1993: 42) notes that Mickiewicz uses as many as 140 terms (excluding rich phraseology) just to name various elements of attire (including hats, shoes, accessories, etc.), and the descriptions of attire perpetuate the image of the vanishing world of nobility in the readers' memory. In fact, Morawski desribed the poem's setting as a time when "there were still many kontuszes, żupans and belts from Słuck in Lithuania" (in Mickiewicz 1971: xiii). Therefore, it can be assumed that the aforementioned outfits are symbols of the entire nobility era.

In addition, clothing plays a very significant role in the poem; it not only provides local color, but it also possesses a specific, ideological significance. Descriptions of the attire worn by a particular character serve as a common literary device: by applying a vivid description of the costume, the poet not only signals the specific beliefs and political views of the described characters, but also expresses their membership in a certain social group (Teodorowicz-Hellman 2006: 371). Clothes depicted in the poem serve to describe particular characters, as they reflect a person's preferences and nature, highlighting and authenticating what the reader learns from the plot. For instance a *kontusz* denotes a patriot, a

---

3   W kontusze, bracia, w kontusze! / bo chcąc być dobrym Polakiem, / Nie dość jest mieć polską duszę, / Potrzeba rozstać się z frakiem.

tailcoat or a frock-coat – a cosmopolitan, and a red collar – a Russian officer. In Soplicowo, wearing a foreign costume is seen as a sign of treason against Poland and Polish customs. One of the characters who condemn "aping" Western attire and lifestyle is the Chamberlain, who considers it as one of the reasons for the loss of independence:

> They damned the dandies but took pattern by them;
> They changed their faith, their costumes, laws and speech.
> That was a masquerade indeed, the breach
> Of a mad time of Carnival, whereafter
> The Lent of slavery would stop all laughter. (Mickiewicz 1962: [1834]: 21)[4]

The tension or even war between the *kontusz* and the frock-coat is clearly visible in *Pan Tadeusz* in the scene when the Notary, normally faithful to the *kontusz*, is forced by his future wife, Telimena, to put on the French frock-coat:

> The Notary then came into the room,
> And said his name, but none could recognise
> The man who hitherto wore Polish guise,
> For Telimena his bride had made him swear
> The Polish kontusz never more to wear.
> Dressed in a French frock-coat, the wretched Pole
> Appeared to have been robbed half his soul.
> He walked as if he'd swallowed a ram-rod,
> And like a crane with awkward movements trod.
> He dared not to look to right or left; 'twas plain
> That though his mien was calm, he was in pain.
> He knew not how to bow, nor what to do
> With those two hands he loved to flourish so!
> And when he tried to tuck them in his belt,
> As he had none, his paunch was all he felt.
> He noticed his mistake; confused he blushed,
> And both inside one pocket quickly pushed.
> He seemed to run the gauntlet of the guests
> Amid their whispered bantering and jests,
> As though ashamed of some disgraceful error.
> He met Matthias' gaze and shook with terror.
>
> Till then the Notary was friend to him,
> But now Matthias looked so fierce and grim,
> He blenched and pulled the coat around him tight,
> As though Matthias might strip it off at sight.

---

4   translated by Watson Kirkconnell.

In fact, he only shouted "Idiot!" twice;
Disgusted by the Notary's new guise,
He rose at once and said goodbye to none,
And slipped out of the castle and was gone. (Mickiewicz 1964/2009 [1834]: 548,550)[5]

The above passage depicts the Notary exposed to ridicule, resentment and even open hostility just because he dared to put on a tailcoat. The contrasting outfits, Polish and foreign, constitute the epitome of the conflict in the work between two ideological attitudes: the patriotic, tied to the native traditions and customs, and the cosmopolitan, vulnerable to foreign influences, especially French, German or English.

The contrast is especially marked as the tailoring of certain elements defined a kind of gesticulation, posture and a way of being. The Notary loved to "flourish" with his hands, which means that he was accustomed to the gesticulation connected with the *kontusz*, and when deprived of his favourite clothes, he is confused and diffident. Gloger (1978: 79–80) provides numerous examples of gestures and habits connected with Old Polish attire, particularly with the *kontusz*: throwing the *wyloty* (i.e. long, loose, slitted sleeves of *kontusz*) on one's back (a sign of readiness for a fight or dance), slapping somebody with *wyloty* (considered an insult), adjusting the *wyloty* (signaling the wish to speak), putting hands behind the belt, etc.

Given the political juxtaposition, Maria Borejszo (2008: 40) notes that clothes described in the poem are, in a way, evaluated. As a rule, the traditional national costumes are assessed very positively. They gain acceptance or even admiration of the ambient of Soplicowo, which is consistent with the spirit and message of the entire work, which, in turn, is an apotheosis of what is irretrievably gone, but still remains in memory to uplift hearts in the time of doubt and sadness. On the other hand, novelties from abroad have rather negative connotations. The criticism of foreign fashion is expressed either explicitly, as in the case of the Chamberlain's monologue on "aping" French fashion in Poland, or indirectly, through a humorous, mocking presentation of characters such as Telimena, the Count, the Cupbearer (Podczaszyc), and the Notary (in the passage about the engagement).

The terms related to Old Polish men's fashion, presented in detail in *Pan Tadeusz*, constitute a significant group of items, and translating them is a great challenge. According to Roman Lewicki (2000: 49), such items belong to "nonequivalent lexis" (*leksyka bezekwiwalentowa*). In this respect, the complex reality

---

5   translated by Kenneth R. Mackenzie.

described by Mickiewicz in *Pan Tadeusz* undergoes inevitable simplifications and distortions in translation.[6]

Ewa Teodorowicz-Hellman (2006: 371) stated that nowadays, for average Polish readers not particularly interested in history, most of the elements of Old Polish attire are not completely comprehensible. However, they induce some associations, evoking images of the Polish nobility customs. These associations are stimulated by illustrations such as Andriolli's drawings for *Pan Tadeusz*, Matejko's paintings, films such as *With Fire and Sword* (*Ogniem i Mieczem*), *The Deluge* (*Potop*), and *Colonel Wolodyjowski* (*Pan Wołodyjowski*), and numerous books and history textbooks referring to the nobility era. Also, knowledge acquired at school plays an important role in understanding terms peculiar to the nobility culture, but an English-speaking reader does not have such cultural competence.

Taking into consideration that Mickiewicz paid particular attention to the old native customs, elements of attire should be treated by a translator with special care and meticulousness. Otherwise, the message of the work will be incomplete. One of the characters of the epic, the Judge, asserts that tradition is the most important factor in re-establishing the Polish state:

> 'By this order', said he, 'homes and nations will flourishAnd with its downfall, houses and nations will perish'.
> (Mickiewicz 2004 [1834], trans. M. Weyland)

Failure to save traditions causes the destruction of nations. Similarly, the failure to preserve the distinctiveness and significance of Old Polish attire in *Pan Tadeusz* results in the complete disappearance of this important cultural aspect, and consequently in making the work less complex and authentic.

The case study

The present case study intends to examine and compare the choices that have been made by seven translators of *Pan Tadeusz* (Maude Ashurst Biggs – 1885, George Rappal Noyes – 1917, Watson Kirkonnell – 1962, Kenneth Mackenzie – 1964, Marcel Weyland – 2004, Leonard Kress – 2006, and Christopher Adam Zakrzewski, who at the moment of writing made six books available on the Internet)

---

6   These types of phenomena were observed by many translation researchers analysing the translations of *Pan Tadeusz*, such as Elżbieta Skibińska (French translation series), Ewa Teodorowicz-Hellman (Swedish translation series), and Katarzyna Lukas (German translation series).

with regard to Old Polish attire. It aims at presenting how the translators strove to overcome the obstacles imposed by untranslatability.

An attempt will be made to identify the global strategy applied by each translator through the examination of particular renderings and the identification of procedures used during their translation, based on Kwieciński's (2001) consolidated taxonomy. Moreover, it will be analyzed whether the translators are consistent in their choices, and whether they have given the reader a possibility to visualize the characteristic gestures, habits and values connected with the attire. In other words, it aims at evaluating whether the translators managed to preserve this important cultural aspect, highlighting the cultural distinctiveness of the source text. On the one hand, they might simplify the message and ignore most of the cultural allusions connected to Old Polish attire to focus on other translation problems; on the other, they ran the risk of employing the original names with insufficient explanation, gambling that the reader will find relevant information elsewhere.

As mentioned before, the lexicon of various elements of attire in *Pan Tadeusz* is made up of 140 words (Krupianka 1993: 42). For this reason, it would be impossible to examine all their renderings in seven translations of the poem within the present work. Therefore, the object of analysis is limited only to terms denoting the most important and frequent Old Polish items of clothing worn by the Polish nobility i.e. *żupan, kontusz, pas kontuszowy, taratatka, czamara, konfederatka, kołpak,* and *opończa.* All these terms will be explained further in the article. Due to the fact that the war between the *kontusz* and the frock-coat is one of the major motifs in *Pan Tadeusz,* the main focus will be on *kontusz.*

Aleksandra Krupianka (1993: 51) defines *kontusz* as a long outer garment girded around the waist with *pas kontuszowy,* worn over a *żupan.* Its characteristic features were *wyloty* i.e. long, loose, slitted sleeves, which could be thrown on the back. Only respected, dignified adults had the right to do so. When someone was slapped with another nobleman's *wyloty,* it was considered an insult. Moreover, throwing *wyloty* on one's back and stroking one's moustache was perceived as a signal of readiness for a fight. In the 1770s Members of Parliament ruled *kontusz* (together with *żupan*) to be a voivodeship uniform, and different voivodeships were obliged to wear differently coloured *kontuszes.*

The first appearance of *kontusz* in *Pan Tadeusz* is a collocation: *wyloty kontusza.*

Widać było z łez, które wylotem kontusza
Otarł prędko, jak kochał pana Tadeusza. (Mickiewicz 2009 [1834]: 15)

The above passage shows the Judge dressed in the traditional Polish *kontusz,* wiping tears with *wyloty* at the moment of welcoming Tadeusz. Unfortunately, none of the translators achieved an adequate effect in translating *wyloty.* Most of the translators (Noyes, Kirkconnell, Mackenzie, Zakrzewski) decided to employ normalization by generalization as they translated *wyloty* as simply "sleeve", or in the case of Zakrzewski "broad sleeve", a slightly more accurate rendering that conveyed the looseness and wideness of *wyloty*. Still, "sleeve" does not express the specificity of this element of attire. Biggs and Weyland applied normalization by modification, choosing "hem" and "lapel" respectively. Both terms denote some kind of border, but are not accurate and include a shift in meaning. Kress, on the other hand, completely deleted this problematic phrase and omitted mention of the garment in his translation of this fragment. In the case of the second element of the collocation, meaning *kontusza*, two choices were made. Biggs and Zakrzewski used normalization by generalization. Biggs chose a very generalized item, "garment", and added an extratextual gloss (in endnotes) where she mentioned that the original word is *kontusz* and provided an explanation of the term. Zakrzewski selected "robe", which is less generalized and seems more adequate as, according to *Oxford Advanced Learner's Dictionary of Current English*, a robe is "a long loose outer piece of clothing, especially one worn as a sign of rank or office at a special ceremony" (Hornby 2005: 1316). Noyes, Kirkconnell and Weyland applied borrowing by importation – *kontusz*; the first two also added explanations in endnotes. Thanks to the consistent usage of the borrowing *kontusz* within the entire epic, the reader is likely to remember this item, and henceforth may associate it with Polish culture.

Wyloty kontusza also appear in a later passage which presents the characteristic gesture connected with that element of *kontusz*: adjusting the *wyloty*. Like in the previous example, the generalized item, "sleeve", prevails as a rendition of *wyloty* (Noyes, Kirkconnell, Zakrzewski); however, Kirkconnell modified the item adding "folds" ("sleeve-folds"). Biggs and Weyland chose normalization by modification again, Weyland using the same rendition as in the previous example – "lapel", whereas Biggs translated *wyloty* as "cuffs". The rendition by Kress is interesting as he removed *wyloty* but added, probably as a kind of compensation, an explanation of the gesture: "straightened out his caftan to show he wished to speak" (Mickiewicz 2006: 13). As for the second part of the collocation, *kontusz*, the procedure of borrowing by importation, *kontusz*, was chosen two times (by Biggs and Noyes), as was deletion (by Kirkconnell and Weyland). Mackenzie and Zakrzewski applied normalization by generalization (Mackenzie – "coat", Zakrzewski – "robe"). Kress used the term "caftan" ("1 a long loose piece of clothing, usually with a belt at the waist, worn by men in Arab countries; 2 a woman's long loose dress with long wide sleeves", Hornby 2005: 841), which can be classified as normalization by modification, as the rendition is not TC-specific yet recognizable for a TT reader.

The last occurrence of *wyloty kontusza* appears in the scene of the Polonaise:

Poloneza czas zacząć. – Podkomorzy rusza
I z lekka zarzuciwszy wyloty kontusza,
I wąsa podkręcając, podał rękę Zosi (Mickiewicz 2009 [1834]: 569)

All of the translators tried to help the reader visualize this scene as they used phrases like "throwing back" (Mackenzie, Kirkconnell, Noyes), "tosses back" (Kress), and "tossing back" (Weyland) to present the Chamberlain's readiness to dance. However, also this time the vast majority of the translators (Noyes, Kirkconnell, Mackenzie, Kress, Weyland) employed normalization by generalization, choosing "sleeve" as a rendition of *wyloty*. Noyes, Kirkconnell, and Mackenzie added an adjective – "flowing", which made the rendition more accurate. Biggs used "cuffs" again, which is an instance of normalization by modification. The borrowing by importation, *kontusz*, was applied by all the translators except Kirkconnell and Mackenzie, who deleted this item from the translation of this collocation. The high frequency of the importation *kontusz* probably results from the willingness of the translators to emphasize the Polishness of the gesture.

Another item connected with *kontusz* is *pas kontuszowy*, which occurs in *Pan Tadeusz* three times. Krupianka (1993: 53–57) describes *pas kontuszowy* as a wide and long cloth sash. Initially, Polish nobles commonly wore leather or woolen sashes, and then richly ornamented silk girdles. There are several typical gestures connected with *pasy kontuszowe*. For instance, when a man wearing a *kontusz* put his hands behind his belt, the gesture displayed pride and self-confidence.

In all the three appearances in *Pan Tadeusz*, *pas* is replaced by either "girdle" or "belt", both items being normalizations by generalization. In most cases, the translators were consistent in their choices, only Noyes and Kirkconnell used these items alternatively. Also, those two translators together with Mackenzie attempted to create recognized exoticism by rendering *pasy konuszowe* as "Polish girdles". As for the second part of the collocation, *kontusz*, Kress is consistent in deleting the costume from the collocation. In turn, Weyland's two first renditions of the phrase are "belt" (normalization by generalization) and "broad belt" (less generalized, highlighting the wideness of *pasy kontuszowe*) with no trace of *kontusz*, while the third instance, "belts from the gentry's kontuszes", not only involves morphologically adapted importation, but also an intratextual gloss ("gentry's" signals the social class).

In the source text, *pas kontuszowy* is mentioned once more, but under another name: *pas słucki*. The adjective *słucki* derives from the most famous Polish manufacture producing *pasy kontuszowe*, located in Słuck. The item was translated into either "belt" (Biggs, Noyes, Kirkconnell, Mackenzie, and Kress) or "sash" (Weyland, Zakrzewski). Although the two choices are significantly different, both of them can be classified as normalization by generalization. Furthermore, each of the translators mentioned the origins of the *pasy*: Mackenzie and Zakrzewski decided to use borrowing by importation ("Słuck"), Noyes, Kirkconnell, Kress, and Weyland also chose borrowing, with orthographic adaptation ("Sluck"). In turn, Biggs tried to follow the original, and attempted at imitating the adjective (*słucki*) and created a phrase "Slucko belt", which was an attempt to create a recognized exoticism.

Apart from the above collocations, *kontusz* itself is mentioned in *Pan Tadeusz* seven times. Some translators, such as Biggs, Noyes, Kirkconnell and Weyland, are very consistent in their choices and preserve the original item (*kontusz*) in all seven instances as they employ borrowing by importation. Also Zakrzewski shows consistency in translating *kontusz* as "robe" (normalization by generalization). However, Mackenzie and Kress choose different renditions depending on the situation.

In the case of a scene depicting mushroom gathering, apart from *kontusz* we encounter *opończa*:

> Dlatego nim ruszyli za Sędzią do lasu,
> Wzięli postawy tudzież ubiory odmienne,
> Służące do przechadzki opończe płócienne,
> Którymi osłaniają po wierzchu kontusze (Mickiewicz 2009 [1834]: 121)

According to Gloger (1978, vol. III: 294), *opończa* is a raincoat, while *Słownik Języka Polskiego* provides a slightly different definition: "an extensive, long, hooded coat with no sleeves, used for travelling" (www.pwn.pl). Mackenzie's normalized description of the clothes depicted in the above passage, "Some o'er their coats put on a linen dress", is a striking generalization. The reader has no opportunity to realize that the apparels are typically Polish, or to understand why a "coat" has to be additionally protected. Kress, for some reason, decided to omit this item and presented the nobility wearing only "canvas capes" (normalization: generalization). As it was mentioned before, the remaining translators preserved the original item (here, in most cases as a morphologically adapted importation – "kontuszes"), which successfully explained why these garments have to be protected during the mushroom gathering. As for *opończa*, Biggs chose "raincloaks of linen", which is a successful normalization by generalization. Noyes and Kirkconnell selected the term "duster", which, according to *Oxford Advanced Learner's Dictionary of Current English,* is an old-fashioned American English word for "a piece of clothing that you wear over your other clothes when you are cleaning the house, etc" (Hornby 2005: 477), which quite accurately covers the meaning of *opończa* (covert cultural substitution). Weyland and Zakrzewski both chose "smock" (which also appropriately conveys the protective purpose of *opończa*) and expanded the rendition: "a smock, long, loose, of unbleached linen" (Weyland), "loose linen smocks" (Zakrzewski), so both translations can be classified as normalizations by generalization (involving diffusion). It seems a good choice to use a domesticating procedure for an item that is not very distinctive and occurs only once in the whole book.

The most important occurrence of *kontusz* can be found in the eleventh book, in the aforementioned scene describing the Notary's and Telimena's engagement, when the cosmopolitan woman forces the man to give up his traditional garments. Apparently, all the translators recognized the significance of the scene, in which the apparel plays the leading role, as all of them preserved the original item, *kontusz*, thus using the procedure of borrowing by importation. What is more, Mackenzie used a distancing device by adding "Polish". No wonder that all the translators chose foreignization because without highlighting the contrast between Polish and foreign costume the scene would be completely incomprehensible. Although the scene is almost at the end of the book, it is the first time Kress and Mackenzie use the original word for *kontusz* in their translations and provide the reader with explicatory glosses (Kress in endnotes, Mackenzie in a footnote).

Before moving on to further occurrences of *kontusz*, it is necessary to provide a definition of *żupan* as the following fragments involve both items. Krupianka (1993: 50) describes *żupan* as a very long garment, often longer than *kontusz*, which was frequently worn over *żupan*. It had tight long sleeves and was fastened at the neck with a loop or a hook and eye. Nowadays, a cassock is a relic of that apparel.

In the first book the Apparitor imagines himself in the court, dressed in Old Polish festive costume comprised of *kontusz* and *żupan*:

I ogląda sam siebie, jak w żupanie białym,
W granatowym kontuszu stał przed trybunałem (Mickiewicz 2009 [1834]: 49)

The first translator, Maude Ashurst Biggs, seems to have rendered this fragment the most faithfully. As for *kontusz*, she used the procedure of borrowing by importation ("kontusz"), while for *żupan* she chose borrowing by orthographically adapted importation ("zupan"). Both the terms are explained in endnotes: *kontusz* is fully explained, but for *żupan* Biggs mentions only that it is "a similar inner garment", which is not a sufficient definition of this term. Noyes and Kirkconnell surprisingly chose the word "smock". *Oxford Advanced Learner's Dictionary of Current English* provides two different definitions of the word "smock". If the translators meant the first one, "a loose comfortable piece of clothing like a long shirt, worn especially by women" (Hornby 2005: 1444), they used normalization by generalization (with a slight modification, as *żupan* was worn exclusively by men). The second meaning, "a long loose piece of clothing worn over other clothes to protect them from dirt", is not appropriate at all (normalization: modification) as *żupan* is a respectable part of the national costume. Moreover, *żupan* was worn either by itself, or under *kontusz*, while the second meaning of smock indicates an outer garment.

In turn, Mackenzie probably wanted to highlight that *żupan* and *kontusz* comprised the national Polish costume and translated these two terms as one: "ancient dress". In this context, with normalization by generalization, such condensed version seems quite acceptable as it presents the traditional character of the apparel. Also Kress normalizes the item by generalization – "dark blue robes".

Weyland's translation, "coat" for *żupan* (generalization: modification), and "kontusz" for *kontusz* (borrowing by importation), is rather strange as it presents the Apparitor wearing two coats, one over the other, one of them being a distinctive Polish coat, and the other a generic one.

Zakrzewski chose "tunic" as a rendition of *żupan*. *Oxford Advanced Learner's Dictionary of Current English* provides three definitions of the term "tunic": first – "a loose piece of clothing covering the body down to the knees, usually without sleeves, as worn in ancient Greece and Rome"; second – "a piece of women's clothing like a tunic, that reaches to the hips and is worn over trousers / pants or a skirt"; third – "(BrE) a tightly fitting jacket worn as part of a uniform by police officers, soldiers, etc" (Hornby 2005: 1649). However, none of them seems to cover the meaning of *żupan*. Therefore, the procedure should be classified as generalization by modification. *Kontusz* is consistently rendered by Zakrzewski as a "robe" (normalization: generalization).

Another scene in which *żupan* and *kontusz* is mentioned depicts Protazy preparing for the road. The following passage emphasizes that *kontusz* and *żupan* are festive attire, not daily clothes:

> Protazy śpieszył włożyć swą woźnieńską odzież:
> Przecież żupana ani kontusza nie kładzie,
> One służą ku wielkiej sądowej paradzie;
> Na podróż ma strój inny (Mickiewicz 2009 [1834]: 267)

In the case of *kontusz*, Biggs, Noyes, Kirkconnell and Weyland ("kontusz" – borrowing by importation), as well as Zakrzewski ("robe" – normalization by generalization) are consistent in their choices, both being quite successful, although importation highlights the national character of the garment. Mackenzie rendered it as "frock", which is an example of overt cultural substitution. Together with Mackenzie's "tunic" for *żupan*, it creates an image of European costumes, while Polishness disappears. Kress, on the other hand, translated *kontusz* as "robber" (generalization, mutation), which must have been an attempt to create a neologism related to 'robe' in order to fit the rhyme. As for *żupan*, there are only two renditions: "zupan", which is a borrowing by orthographically adapted importation (Biggs), and "tunic", which is normalization by modification (Noyes, Kirkconnell, Mackenzie, Weyland, Kress, and Zakrzewski).

The Polish costume of *kontusz* and *żupan* was officially made voivodeship uniform in the 1770s. In such capacity the items occur in the scene presenting the Chamberlain after the mass:

> Miał mundur województwa: żupan złotem szyty,
> Kontusz gredyturowy z frędzlą i pas lity,
> Przy którym karabela z głownią jaszczurową;
> Na szyi świecił wielką szpinką brylantową;
> Konfederatka biała, a na niej pęk gruby
> Drogich piórek, były to białych czapel czuby (Mickiewicz 2009 [1834]: 497)

In the case of *kontusze*, Biggs, quite surprisingly, preserves the original spelling of the ST item – "kontusze" in the plural form (borrowing, importation). Noyes, Kirkconnell, and Weyland employ borrowing by morphologically adapted importation, "kontuszes", while Mackenzie and Kress choose normalization by generalization: "coat" and "robe" respectively.

Renderings of *żupan* in the scene are identical as before: Biggs consistently uses "zupan", and the rest of the translators – "tunic".

The above passage also contains a term for headgear typical at that time – *konfederatka*. According to Gloger (1978: 76), *konfederatka* was a high square-top cap, often crimson or navy blue, trimmed with black, grey or chestnut sheepskin, often decorated with heron feathers, made famous and named for members of the Bar Confederation. Apart from the above fragment, *konfederatka* occurs in the book four more times. The translators rendered it in four ways, with a total of 36 renderings throughout the whole set of translations; it appeared as "cap" (normalization by generalization, used 18 times in total), "hat" (normalization by modification, used 6 times), "confederate cap" (recent TL-modelled coinage, used 6 times), and "square-top hat" (normalization by modification, used once). None of the translators is consistent in their choices within the whole book. Also, none of them regarded *konfederatka* as significant enough to provide an explanation for this item.

Another headgear depicted by Mickiewicz is *kołpak*, which was a kind of a soft high cap often faced with fur. It was slightly wider at the top than at the bottom, or cylindrical, worn by both men and women. In 1790 *kołpak* became an official headgear of Polish infantry. (Gloger 1978: 62) There are two appearances of this item in *Pan Tadeusz*: "Ostatni król co nosił kołpak Witoldowy" (Mickiewicz 2009 [1834]: 153) and "Stał ułan jak słonecznik w błyszczącym kołpaku" (Mickiewicz 2009 [1834]: 501).

Both the occurrences are very culture-specific. The first passage evokes the ancient rite of crowning a new prince of the Grand Duchy of Lithuania with *kołpak*. The second one presents an uhlan (a member of Polish light cavalry) wearing this headgear. Therefore, *kołpak* should be treated with special attention. However, the translators tend to normalize this item, especially in the first instance. Noyes, Mackenzie, Kress, Weyland and Zakrzewski chose "cap" (normalization, generalization) as a rendition of the first appearance of *kołpak*. Kirkconnell also used normalization by generalization but his rendition – "bearskin cap" – is slightly more specific and adequate. Biggs, in both instances, chose borrowing by orthographically adapted importation – "kolpak", and provided a short explanation of the item in a footnote. The second mention of this headgear was probably recognized as more relevant since the translators demonstrate more creativity, albeit with varying success. Kirkconnell and Weyland employ the procedure of recognized exoticism, limited normalization as they translate *kołpak* as shako (tall military cap). Noyes and Kress chose "head-dress", which is a normalization by modification. The most inadequate interpretation seems to be the one by Mackenzie, who rendered *kołpak* (a soft cap) as "helmet", which is an obvious mutation.

The next passage presents Kościuszko taking an oath on the first day of the Kościuszko Uprising. Mickiewicz depicted him dressed in traditional Polish clothes:

> Wielki człowiek! a chodził w krakowskiej sukmanie,
> To jest czamarce' – 'W jakiej czamarce, Mospanie?
> Odparł Wilbik, to przecież zwano taratatką.'
> 'Ale tamta z frędzlami, ta jest całkiem gładką'
> Krzyknął Mickiewicz; – zatem wszczynały się swary
> O różnych taratatki kształtach i czamary. (Mickiewicz 2009 [1834]: 173)

Czamara and *taratatka* are quite similar apparels. *Taratatka* (Krupianka 1993: 49) was a capote commonly worn in eighteenth century Poland, reaching to the knees, with 'needs' (such as ribbons, buttons, lapels etc.), while *czamara* (Krupianka 1993: 47) was a long outer Persian dress with long sleeves, with buttons, fastened up to the neck. The above passage, depicting characters who do not remember the exact appearance of *taratatka* and *czamara*, serves to emphasize that the nobility era is on the wane. Only one character, deliberately called Mickiewicz, seems able to differentiate between these clothes. The importance of these garments was recognized by all the translators, and Biggs, Noyes and Kirkconnell provided the reader with explanations. In the translation of this passage Biggs and Noyes use importations exclusively. Moreover, Biggs even uses the original spelling and plural forms ("considering taratatki and czamary"). In addition, Zakrzewski, Kress, Noyes, and Biggs use distancing devices (italics) when applying the borrowing. Also the other translators in most cases rely on the procedure of borrowing by importation but their translations differ in the rendering of the last line of the fragment ("O różnych taratatki kształtach i czamary"). Kirkconnell's "these jackets" can be recognized as normalization by modification. Mackenzies's "coat and cloak", as well as Weyland's "different apparels" are normalizations by generalization. Zakrzewski's rendition of the pair of items, "frock and coat" (particularly the first element), can be considered as overt cultural substitution. In turn, Kress simplifies his translation with a partial deletion:

> I saw Kosciuszko, our nation's commander,
> dressed in a Cracow peasant coat. In truth
> they [call, *sic*] it a *czamara* like that of the Hussar."
> "It certainly was not," Wilbik retorted—
> as the querulous factions quarreled again. (Mickiewicz 2006 [1834]: 78)[7]

The figure of Kościuszko appears also at the very beginning of the book and is depicted at the moment of announcing the general uprising in 1794 (later called Kościuszko Uprising):

> Tu Kościuszko w czamarce krakowskiej, z oczyma
> Podniesionymi w niebo, miecz oburącz trzyma;
> Takim był, gdy przysięgał na stopniach ołtarzów,
> Że tym mieczem wypędzi z Polski trzech mocarzów
> Albo sam na nim padnie. (Mickiewicz 2009 [1834]: 5)

However, here the approach of the translators is completely different as only Biggs decided to use foreignization (borrowing by importation – "czamara"). Biggs, as well as Noyes and Kirkconnell, added explicatory glosses. The vast majority of the translators chose normalization by generalization – "coat" (Noyes, Kirkconnell, Mackenzie, and Zakrzewski). Kress selected "dress", which is also normalization by generalization, while Weyland's "cap" is normalization by mutation as czamara

---

7   translation by Leonard Kress.

is obviously not a cap. What is more, each rendition is accompanied by the adjective *krakowski* appearing in various forms (Cracovian, Cracow, Kraków). This 'national' label makes the translations look more like recognized exoticisms.

It is quite surprising that in this case foreignization is adopted only by Biggs, while in the previous example all the translators tended to do the same. Some might have been aware that Mickiewicz made a mistake – Kościuszko was not dressed in *czamara* during the oath, but actually in a general's uniform. Stanisław Pigoń noticed that he began to wear this peasant clothing only after the Battle of Racławice to honour the scythebearers (Krupianka 1993: 47).

Finally, the last excerpt under analysis depicts as many as four traditional garments in one scene, presenting Polish nobles imprisoned by Russian soldiers. The Russian Major commands to strip them of their Polish clothing:

> Kazał pierwej pozdzierać z głów konfederatki,
> Z pleców płaszcze, kontusze, nawet taratatki,
> Nawet żupany. (Mickiewicz 2009 [1834]: 387)

All the renditions of *konfederatka* were normalized: Biggs, Noyes, Mackenzie, and Weyland chose generalization – "caps", while Kirkconnell and Kress selected modification – "hats". As for *kontusze*, Noyes, Kirkconnell, and Weyland used the morphologically adapted importation "kontuszes". Biggs, on the other hand, again preserved the original Polish spelling "kontusze". Mackenzie's "coat" is a normalization by generalization. The translations of *taratatka* are mostly normalizations by modification, with a dominance of "jacket" (Noyes, Kirkconnell, Mackenzie), and one instance of "waistcoat" by Weyland. For the last item, *żupany*, all the translators selected different renderings. Kirkconnell's "under-smock" seems to have been an attempt at naturalization by modification. However, this compound is probably striking for a native speaker, which makes it the closest to a new coinage. Biggs invariably relies on borrowing (in this case, orthographically adapted – "zupan"). Noyes, Mackenzie and Weyland employ normalization by modification (Noyes – "tunic", Mackenzie – "undercoat", Weyland – "vest"). Finally, Kress renders all the three apparels by "coats and tunics", which is normalization by generalization with condensation, bordering on deletion. Therefore, only Biggs's renditions make the reader visualize the defeated Polish nobility dressed in patriotic Old Polish costumes.

General observations and conclusions

The first translator of *Pan Tadeusz*, Maude Ashurst Biggs, relied on foreignization. In most cases she is faithful to the procedure of borrowing by importation. In every situation where Biggs preserved the original item, she employed a distancing device in the form of italics. Moreover, she provided an explanation to all the apparels under the present discussion (excluding *konfederatka*), so it seems that she decided to save the local color, but at the same time enabled the reader to understand it. As a devotee of Polish culture, she was very scrupulous in her renditions. The audience of her translation has the opportunity to get to know Old Polish fashion and customs connected to it.

The image of Old Polish attire in the translations by George Rapall Noyes and Watson Kirkconnell is very similar; in fact, Kirkconnell admitted in the preface to his translation that he made use of the prose translation of his older colleague (Mickiewicz 1962: vii). They both endeavoured to find a 'golden mean' between domestication and foreignization. When they used exoticizing procedures they usually included explanatory glosses. Both the translators recognized the significance of *kontusz* in *Pan Tadeusz* and the need to preserve the original item in order to highlight its uniqueness. However, they did not ascribe the same value to *żupan*. In each fragment depicting both *kontusz* and *żupan* (e.g. as a festive national dress or the uniform of the voivodeship), they created a strange image of the characters wearing a typically Polish garment over an ordinary one (smock or tunic). Nevertheless, generally speaking, their choices are quite adequate and consistent.

Kenneth R. Mackenzie's translation, although beautiful and pleasurable, on closer analysis reveals weaknesses in the form of inconsistent choices (probably due to the pressure to fit the rhyme) and oversights (such as the translation of *kołpak* as "helmet"). In relation to clothes, he often used very general vocabulary. His rather domesticated translation of attire deprived *Pan Tadeusz* of its distinctiveness, and therefore some aspects of the message are lost in translation. Notwithstanding, the 2009 edition of Mackenzie's translation contains Michał Elwiro Andriolli's illustrations for *Pan Tadeusz*, which realistically present the attire, so what is lost in his translation can be transferred by illustrations.

Marcel Weyland, with his tendency to foreignize, did not allow his readership to have a full grasp of Old Polish attire as he provided explanations only for *kontusz* and *pas słucki*, leaving the other foreignized items incomprehensible for the target audience at first sight. His attempts at normalization sometimes involve radical shifts of meaning (such as his rendition of *czamara* as "cap"), revealing certain gaps in his knowledge of Old Polish costumes. Although not flawless, his translation of attire is rather consistent and a careful reader shall be able to get to know Old Polish fashion to some extent.

Leonard Kress tends to simplify his translation by frequent use of the domesticating procedure of deletion. Perhaps he did not consider the attire relevant enough for the effort of comprehension required from the target reader. Kress used foreignization only when it was absolutely indispensible (e.g. in the fragment about the Notary's engagement costume). The reader has almost no chance to realize the specificity of Old Polish attire. Therefore, the translation fails to preserve one of the most significant cultural layers of *Pan Tadeusz*.

Judging by those six books available at the time of writing, Christopher Adam Zakrzewski tends to domesticate terms connected with attire. Notwithstanding, he uses exoticizing strategies when the context requires it (e.g. in the case of the quarrel about *taratatka* and *czamara*). Zakrzewski provides no explanatory notes.

The overall bias of the entire corpus of translations is towards domestication, and many important cultural matters are lost in translation.

Foreignizing strategies would seem to be the most natural option when the translated work is so immersed in culture that it attains the status of a national symbol like in the case of *Pan Tadeusz*. Through this strategy the reader is able to notice and appreciate the cultural separateness and uniqueness of the source culture. However, preserving an original item is not enough as the described reality may be incomprehensible. The reader should not be deprived of the possibility to learn about a foreign culture. Such educational function can be performed by paratext (such as footnotes, forewords, endnotes, glossaries, etc), as well as embedded glosses. Many translators avoid using paratextual glosses and they treat them as a 'necessary evil'. The present writer believes that they do not disrupt the pleasure of reading since if the reader wishes, they can simply ignore them and enjoy the encounter with otherness. Moreover, any type of explanatory gloss seems to be a sign that the translator respects the reader. As a result of such a combination of procedures (borrowing and normalization by gloss), the foreign culture of the source text does not perish in the target text. In keeping with the suggestions of Lawrence Venuti (1995: 21), such a translation behavior would contribute to the reduction of cultural asymmetry, especially when the source culture is weaker than the target culture, as in the case of Polish vs. British or American culture.

Readers' reception of the translations: a questionnaire

For the purposes of the present study, a questionnaire has been given to twenty native speakers of English of different ages and various levels of education to examine the effect of particular renderings on the potential readers of *Pan Tadeusz*; more specifically, to test whether the reader is able to notice the distinctiveness of the source culture.

In the task in question the respondents were presented with eight excerpts from *Pan Tadeusz* depicting attire, from various English translations of *Pan Tadeusz*.

Excerpts 1, 2, 5, 7 involved domesticated renditions of Old Polish garments, and fragments 3, 6, 8 – foreignized ones. Excerpt 4 portrayed European costumes. The respondents were asked to identify whether the attire worn by the described character is Polish (typical of Polish nobility) or European.

Figure 1: Recognition of Polish and European clothes on the basis of translation excepts

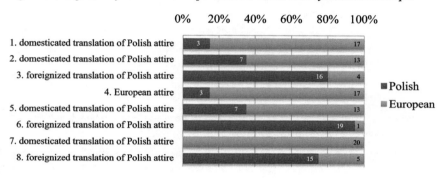

The data gathered shows that Polish garments depicted in the foreignized extracts were mostly correctly perceived by the respondents as Polish, and these described in the domesticated ones as European. Therefore, it appears that the reader notices the cultural distinctiveness much more clearly when the translator uses the foreignizing strategy.

Conclusion

The study has shown that domesticated representations of Old Polish attire prevail in the English translation series of *Pan Tadeusz*. As a result, the specificity of Polish traditional costumes disappears from most of the translations. The only version retaining the full image of attire and highlighting the contrast between Polish and foreign costumes, which is so important in the book, is the one by Maude Ashurst Biggs. Unfortunately, this translation is hardly available as it was published in 1885. Therefore, the English-speaking reader does not have the opportunity to fully appreciate the distinctiveness of this cultural layer of *Pan Tadeusz*. The simplification or modification of the content may contribute to a lower assessment of Mickiewicz's work, which, in translation, may be reduced to an ordinary love story.

All things considered, it appears that foreignizing strategies accompanied by explanatory glosses are the best solution to allow the reader to understand the alien culture, but at the same time detect its distinctiveness and uniqueness. As a result of domestication, the reader is deprived of the possibility to learn the full cultural message of a work, and certain aspects of a particular culture to be lost in translation. Of course, a translator is not a miracle-worker, and even the best and the most adequate translation will not grant the target text the same position in a different culture as the one occupied by the original within the source culture. In addition, it should be stressed that the role of illustrations in any work rich with cultural connotations cannot be overestimated. Drawings and pictures may dispel the reader's doubts about the depicted realities, as well as correct any false impressions. Therefore, illustrations should not be treated only as decorations, but as an integral part of comments and notes.

References

Bartkiewicz, Magdalena. 1979. *Polski ubiór do 1864 roku*. Wrocław: Zakład Narodowy im. Ossolińskich.

Borejszo, Maria. 2008. "Obraz mody w *Panu Tadeuszu*", in Beata Gromadzka, Dorota Mrozek, and Jerzy Kaniewski (eds.) *Kultura – Język – Edukacja: Dialogi współczesności z tradycją*, 231–244.

Chlebowski, Bronisław. 1917. *Rozwój kultury polskiej w treściwym zarysie przedstawiony*. Warszawa: Gebethner i Wolff.

Debska, Anita. 2000. *Country of the mind. An introduction to the poetry of Adam Mickiewicz*. Warszawa: Burchard Edition.

Gloger, Zygmunt. 1978. *Encyklopedia staropolska ilustrowana*. Warszawa: Wiedza Powszechna.

Hornby, Albert, S. 2005 [1948] *Oxford advanced learner's dictionary of current English*. Oxford: University Press.

Krupianka, Aleksandra. 1993. "Ze studiów nad słownictwem *Pana Tadeusza* Adama Mickiewicza: Słownictwo ubioru szlacheckiego". *Acta Universitatis Nicolai Copernici (276)*, 1993, 41–59.

Kwieciński, Piotr. 2001. *Disturbing Strangeness: Foreignisation and domestication intranslation procedures in the context of cultural asymmetry*. Toruń: Wydawnictwo Edytor.

Labuda, Aleksander Wit. 1993. "Pan Tadeusz we francuskiej tradycji przekładowej" *Pamiętnik Literacki* LXXXIV, 63–74.

Lewicki, Roman. 2000. *Obcość w odbiorze przekładu*. Lublin: Wydawnictwo Uniwersytetu Marii Curie-Skłodowskiej.

Mickiewicz, Adam. 2011. "Book one: The manor", trans. Christopher Adam Zakrzewski. *The Sarmatian Review,* http://www.ruf.rice.edu/~sarmatia/110/301mickie.htm, DOA: March 22, 2011.

Mickiewicz, Adam. 2011. "Book two: The castle", trans. Christopher Adam Zakrzewski. *The Sarmatian Review,* http://www.ruf.rice.edu/~sarmatia/908/283mickie.htm, DOA: March 22, 2011.

Mickiewicz, Adam. 2011. "Book three: Coquetries", trans. Christopher Adam Zakrzewski. *The Sarmatian Review,* http://www.ruf.rice.edu/~sarmatia/410/302zakrze.pdf, DOA: March 22, 2011.

Mickiewicz, Adam. 2011. "Book four", trans. Christopher Adam Zakrzewski. *The Sarmatian Review,* http://www.ruf.rice.edu/~sarmatia/400/mickiewicz.html, DOA March 22, 2011.

Mickiewicz, Adam. 2011. "Book five: The quarrel", trans. Christopher Adam Zakrzewski. *The Sarmatian Review,* http://www.ruf.rice.edu/~sarmatia/910/303mickie-zakrze.pdf, DOA March 22, 2011.

Mickiewicz, Adam. 2011. "Book six: The gentry village", trans. Christopher Adam Zakrzewski. *The Sarmatian Review,* http://www.ruf.rice.edu/~sarmatia/111/111zakrze.pdf, DOA March 22, 2011.

Mickiewicz, Adam. 1885. *Master Thaddeus; Or, the last foray in Lithuania: An historical epic poem in 12 books. Vol. 1,* trans. Maude Ashurst Biggs. London: Trübner.

Mickiewicz, Adam. 1885. *Master Thaddeus; Or, the last foray in Lithuania: An historical epic poem in 12 books. Vol. 2,* trans. Maude Ashurst Biggs. London: Trübner.

Mickiewicz, Adam. 1949 [1917]. *Pan Tadeusz,* trans. George Rapall Noyes. London: J.M. Dent & Sons Ltd.

Mickiewicz, Adam. 1962. *Pan Tadeusz or the last foray in Lithuania,* trans. Watson Kirkconnell. New York: The Polish Institute of Arts and Sciences in America.

Mickiewicz, Adam. 2009 [1964]. *Pan Tadeusz or the last foray in Lithuania,* trans. Kenneth R. Mackenzie. Łomianki: Wydawnictwo LTW.

Mickiewicz, Adam. 1971 [1834]. *Pan Tadeusz czyli ostatni zjazd na Litwie. Historia szlachecka z roku 1811 i 1812 we dwunastu księgach wierszem.* Wrocław: Zakład Narodowy im. Ossolińskich.

Mickiewicz, Adam. 2004. *Pan Tadeusz or the last foray in Lithuania: A tale of gentry during 1811–1812,* trans. Marcel Weyland. http://www.antoranz.net/BIBLIOTEKA/PT051225/-PanTad-eng/PT-Start.htm, DOA: February 18, 2011.

Mickiewicz, Adam. 2006. *Pan Tadeusz or the last Foray in Lithuania: A history of the nobility in the years 1811 and 1812 in twelve books of verse*, trans. Leonard Kress. Harrow Gate Press, http://leonardkress.com/Pan%20Tadeusz.pdf, DOA: February 18, 2011.

Miłosz, Czesław. 1969. *The history of Polish literature*. London: The Macmillan Company; Collier Macmillan.

Skibińska, Elżbieta. 2006. "Literacka etnografia, czyli świat kultury *Pana Tadeusza* w opiniach historyków literatury", in Bogusław Dopart (ed.) *Pan Tadeusz i jego dziedzictwo. Recepcja*, 249–267.

Słownik Języka Polskiego, http://www.pwn.pl/?module=multisearch&search=opo%F1cza&-submit2=szukaj, DOA June 8, 2011.

Tazbir, Janusz. 1978. *Kultura szlachecka w Polsce: Rozkwit, upadek, relikty* Warszawa: Wiedza Powszechna.

Teodorowicz-Hellman, Ewa. 2006. "*Pan Tadeusz* w przekładzie na język szwedzki. Forma utworu, tytuły szlacheckie, polski strój narodowy", in Bogusław Dopart (ed.) *Pan Tadeusz i jego dziedzictwo. Recepcja*, 349–380.

Venuti, Lawrence. 1995. *The translator's invisibility*. London and New York: Routledge.

Krzysztof Wadyński

From the Wild Fields to the DVD.
A domesticating approach in the translation
of *With Fire and Sword*

Ogniem i mieczem (*With Fire and Sword*), written by a Nobel prize winner Henryk Sienkiewicz, is an all-time classic novel for the Polish culture, bearing the collective name 'Trilogy' along with its continuations, *The Deluge* and *Fire in the Steppe*. It was published in 1884 in the era of partitions so that Poles would not forget about their lost motherland and still hope for the independence of Poland. Since then it has become one of the most read and recognizable books in the Polish culture and has been translated into many foreign languages. So far the book has been translated into English twice, by Jeremiah Curtin and by Wiesław S. Kuniczak. In 1999, J. Hoffman directed a film on the basis of *With Fire and Sword*, which was rendered into English by Elżbieta Gałązka-Salamon, whose translation is not based on either of the literary translations.

It is crucial to mention that both in the film and in the book the existence of culture-specific items reflects the specificity and uniqueness of the lands and cultures seen by both the readers and the viewers. The aim of this paper is to examine the film translation and see what strategies and procedures have been used by the translator with regard to culture-specific items, and describe the consequences of such choices. It will analyze whether the translator used procedures connected to the notion of foreignization, to expose the viewers to exotic elements and include local flavour, or domestication procedures, in order to hide the strangeness and stress what is universal about the film as an adventure movie.

The analysis of the rendering of the film *With Fire and Sword* was conducted on the basis of both Polish and English subtitles included in the DVD version of the film and additionally supplied by a few examples transcribed from the dialogues themselves, when the Polish subtitles proved to be insufficient.

It should be mentioned that the film itself was created to stress the specific multiculturalism of the region and allow viewers to see how various cultures mixed, coexisted and sometimes fought with each other. In order to achieve that goal, the producers invited a multi-national cast, incorporated several languages and stressed Ukraine's struggle for independence. Bearing that in mind, the list of examples below includes only those elements whose rendering proved particularly difficult or controversial.

Forms of address in the film translation

Forms of address are among the most culturally significant elements. Their purpose in the past in the Polish language was not only to designate interlocutors but to present one's attitude towards him or her and one's own social position. However, in the translation of the film created by Gałązka-Salamon the most noticeable procedure with respect to these forms was to avoid them by deletion. The following section will present procedures used to render particular terms and forms of address.

Rycerze is a form of address which could be directly translated as 'Knights'; in theory, all Polish noblemen, poor or rich alike, could call themselves 'Knights', as they were all supposed to be equal. In the 17th century, the term did not possess any real significance and was used only to stress the bravery and other virtues of men of noble blood. It the film this term is used in two types of situations. First of all, it is used as a cry for help in a situation that fits a "damsels in distress" scenario. To match the situation, the translator chose 'Chevaliers!' as an equivalent, to stress the similarity of such a scene to a medieval romance. On the other hand, in all other situations 'Rycerze' was translated into 'Gentlemen', which transformed a very polite and old-fashioned way to address another nobleman into a standard, generic one, that can be easily absorbed by the viewer. Additionally, the "knightly" virtues of honour, bravery, and combat prowess disappear from such a form of address, substituted by less marked values such as civility and proper manners.

Pan was the universal and polite form used to address another nobleman of equal status; hence the main protagonists are called 'Pan Skrzetuski', 'Pan Zagłoba', 'Pan Wołodyjowski' etc. 'Pan' could be used both in an informal conversation and in more formal situations, unless a nobleman possessed another title, which then replaced 'Pan'. In this case the translator of the film decided to use the normalization procedure and render 'Pan' by means of two options. First of all, all of the noblemen who are professional soldiers are addressed as Sir, e.g. Sir John Skrzetuski or Sir Longinus, but in contrast with them is Mr. Zagłoba, who is a civilian nobleman and who decides to serve under Jeremi Wiśniowiecki on his own. This distinction is not explicitly addressed in the film, which can result in the viewer wondering whether the other noblemen are being disrespectful towards Zagłoba. Unlike 'Pan', 'Sir' is only used with the first name and perhaps this is the reason why the first and the middle name of Zagłoba (Jan Onufry) are lost in translation; otherwise, 'Sir John' would appear twice, referring to two different characters. Another key character, Longinus Podbipięta, a Lithuanian nobleman of great strength, is introduced by Zagłoba with his full name as well as his coat of arms in the original text, and throughout the film he is mostly referred to as 'pan Podbipięta'. However, the translator decided to use the procedure of deletion and remove his surname altogether. Therefore, he is referred to as either 'Sir Longinus' or 'Hoodsnatcher', which is the name of his coat of arms. The possible explanation of this procedure is that it seemed unnecessary to use his surname, as the form 'Sir Longinus' was sufficient; however, it did not seem to be the case concerning other significant characters in the story, such as Skrzetuski or Wołodyjowski.

Terms such as *waszmość, jegomość, waćpanna,* or *mości panowie* were commonly used by noblemen while addressing men and women of status equal to their own. They were a crucial element of a conversation, showing respect towards a fellow noble. The range of usage was very wide, from more formal situations to informal meetings among acquaintances. In this case the translator made the decision to delete the terms altogether, probably due to the lack of available equivalents. Characters refer to others using the pronoun 'you', which can also be used in both formal and informal situations. The only exception from this is the use of 'Gentlemen!' when translating 'Mości Panowie!', used to respectfully address noblemen and attract their attention.

Another form of address, *Jaśnie oświecony,* was used in formal situations towards a group of high-born noblemen who by means of birth and career managed to achieve the status of the most influential men in the country. The group contained senators, princes, dukes, voivodes, hetmans etc. In two situations the term is translated in two different ways. In the first example, when it is used by a drunken Cossack who appropriates the title, the translator decided to use the procedure of normalization (by generalization) and the end product was 'magnate', which is a good way to describe the social standing of the aforementioned group. However, in the second example the term needed to be used as an official title ("Jaśnie Oświecony Książę Wojewodo") and the translator decided to use a calque ('Your Enlightened Excellency Prince and Governor').

Towards noblemen of higher social status the form *wielmożny* or *jaśnie wielmożny* was used more formally in documents and letters as a title, and in spoken situations during official meetings. The translator produced two different versions of these terms. In both cases she tried to use the procedure of covert cultural substitution. 'Wielmożny' was translated into 'His Excellency', a title defined by the *Oxford Dictionaries Online* as "a title or form of address given to certain high officials of state, especially ambassadors, or of the Roman Catholic Church". In view of the definition, this example can be considered as a rather good equivalent. However, the analogous form 'Jaśnie Wielmożny', which was used in the scene when drunken Cossacks boast about their victory and imagine themselves with new titles, was translated into 'His Highness', a title given to persons of royal rank. As a result, a viewer might be under the impression that every nobleman who bears a significant title in the Polish-Lithuanian Commonwealth is a member of the royal family.

Wasza Książęca Mość refers to the heads of the dynasties who possessed great power in the Polish-Lithuanian Commonwealth and whose lineage could be traced back to Polish, Lithuanian or Ruthenian dukes, e.g. the Rurykowicz or the Giedyminowicz family. The translator decided to translate the phrase as 'Excellency'. The same term was used to render the term 'Wielmożny', and we can assume that it is a normalization (generalization) procedure. Unfortunately, by such a generalization, a prince is reduced to the status of a rich nobleman – a status that could be achieved by any nobleman in the Commonwealth rather than be related to "ancient" blood.

Najjaśniejszy Panie and *Miłościwy Panie/Królu* were forms of address used only when addressing the king in conversations and letters. In the film, the occurrence of these forms can only be noticed during one of the final scenes when the long-absent king finally appears. Initially he is addressed as 'Najjaśniejszy Panie' by the Chancellor and a courtier. The translator decided to delete all occurrences of this title and replace it every time simply by 'you', seemingly lowering the position of the king. Since in the scene the king is not wearing a crown and is dressed in plain Western clothes, the rendering might cause confusion concerning the role and social status of this new character. In the second part of the scene the king is referred to as 'Miłościwy Panie/Królu' by a servant and by Skrzetuski, whose status is that of a simple solider. In this case the translator decided to use a cultural equivalent and chose to use 'Your majesty', which in English is a term reserved solely for the ruling monarch.

Maty!, a term used by Bohun to address Helena's mother, can be directly translated from Ukrainian as 'mother', which shows the relationship between the Cossack officer and the Ruthenian noble family; the feelings appear to be mutual as Helena's mother states that she treats him as a foster son. Removing this element from the film leaves Bohun only in the role of a family companion and reduces the impact of later tragic events.

Military terminology

As the subject of the film is civic war, many terms of address and other culture-specific items are connected to the military.

Bat'ku [hetmane] is used by Cossacks to address their leader, Bohdan Chmielnicki. This phrase is a combination of an official, military form of address, as 'hetman' refers to a commander of the army, and of deep, almost family-like feelings towards the leader, as *Bat'ko* (Батько) can be directly translated from Ukrainian into English as 'father'. In this way the Cossack masses express their bond and trust in the leadership and skills of the leader of the uprising. With the deletion of this phrase, one of the crucial cultural features of the Cossack army and, by extension, of their cause, disappears.

Panie namiestniku is the manner in which Rzędzian refers to the main protagonist, Skrzetuski, in one of the opening scenes of the film. 'Namiestnik' or "namiestnik chorągwi pancernej" is indeed the protagonist's military rank. This rank has not been used in the Polish military for a long time, but in the 17th and 18th century it referred to a commander of a 'chorągiew' in the absence of a lieutenant or a 'rotmistrz'. In the film the term is translated as "lieutenant", thus making it an example of covert cultural substitution. In the ST, Skrzetuski's rank was below a lieutenant (or a first lieutenant if we decide to make that distinction) and only later does he manage to become a lieutenant. Therefore this rendering is slightly inaccurate with respect to military terminology.

The antagonist, Bohun, is referred to as *podpułkownik*. This military rank refers to the second-in-command after a 'pułkownik', thus making him a high-ranking officer in a regiment. The names of these two military ranks, 'podpułkownik' and 'pułkownik', have not changed over the years. In the film the translator rendered 'podpułkownik' as 'colonel'. In this example, there is a similar inaccuracy as in the previous one. The standard translation of 'podpułkownik' is 'Lieutenant Colonel', but just as it was in the previous example, it is a longer form. Judging from these two examples, it might be assumed that the translator chose those particular renderings to save space in the subtitles, even at the cost of historical and military accuracy.

Another rank, *wachmistrz*, refers to a low-ranking officer in a cavalry unit and it corresponded to a sergeant of infantry in the armies of the Polish-Lithuanian Commonwealth. The difference between these terms was introduced to make a clear distinction between the two types of armies. Gałązka-Salamon produced a more unified and modern translation, namely 'sergeant'. Even though it is a functional equivalent of this rank, there is a sense of cultural loss in presenting 17th c. soldiers with a modern unified ranks.

Ataman koszowy was a high-ranking officer in the Cossack army who held both political and military functions, being in charge of the 'kosz', i.e. military encampment. He was either the supreme commander or the second-in-command after the hetman. English-speaking historians use this term as a recognized exoticism, spelling it as either 'kosh otaman' or 'kosh ataman'. In the English translation of the film, we are presented with 'Chief Ataman': 'ataman' is retained as a recognized exoticism but the introduction of 'Chief' might cause some confusion concerning the commanders' order of precedence and Chmielnicki's place in it.

Another military term, *pospolite ruszenie*, refers to the Commonwealth's military force that was summoned in times of crisis and consisted exclusively of Polish and Lithuanian noblemen and their servants. Depending on the level of threat the force could be called from either one voivodeship or the whole country. Therefore, noblemen from regions which were under constant threat from e.g. Russians or Tartars were a notable military force, while those who came from peaceful voivodeships like Wielkopolska were of little battle utility. In the translation presented by Gałązka-Salamon, covert cultural substitution is used and thus viewers are presented with 'militia' as an equivalent to this term. At first glance, the terms seem equivalent; however, the target term does not specify whether the force raised consists of all men who are able to bear arms, as it was in the middle ages and later during the French Revolution, or only of noblemen, as it was in the case of 'pospolite ruszenie'. Therefore, the result presented to the viewers might lead to a misunderstanding of the organization of the Polish-Lithuanian army.

Social culture and organization

The above military terms are inextricably bound with the history and structure of the whole country, a topic which, although not explicitly discussed in the film, surfaces in numerous mentions of offices, authorities, historic figures and events.

In the context of the film, *Rzeczpospolita* is the name of the state which emerged after the Union of Lublin in 1569 between the Crown of Poland and the Great Duchy of Lithuania. In the translation the term 'Commonwealth' is used a few times, but the dominant translation is 'Poland'. This may be described as a procedure of normalization by specification, as the whole of the action in the film is set in lands belonging to the Crown of Poland; however, it might be seen as either historical inaccuracy, or even a method of showing the supremacy of the Crown which could be offensive to Lithuanians, since the state was officially a union of two nations (*Rzeczpospolita Obojga Narodów*).

The matter is crucial for the plot. Speaking to Skrzetuski, Bohdan Chmielnicki defends his rebellion against the Commonwealth by blaming magnates in the following way: "A gdyby nie oni, *miałaby Rzeczpospolita nie Dwojga a Trojga narodów* tysiące szabel". In this speech he points out that the very crux of the uprising is the oppression of Ruthenians, and that Ruthenian lands should not be treated as a part of the Crown of Poland, but as a separate political body in the union, with equal privileges. The translation of this example ("It's because of them Ukraine won't join your Alliance") changes the meaning of the sentence. First of all, there was no alliance between Poland and Lithuania, but a union. Moreover, it was not a matter of Ukraine joining it, as it was already in it, but rather a matter of reforming it in order to suit the demands of the Cossacks. Additionally, "Ukraine won't" suggests that Ukraine does not wish to be a part of the Commonwealth, while the Polish version suggests the very opposite: they are prevented from participating on equal terms by the Polonized magnates. As a result, the English version implies a rebellion against the king, which is precisely what the speaker denies.

The magnates in question are *królewięta*: a limited group of noblemen who possessed massive wealth and areas of land in the voivodeships of modern-day Ukraine. They enjoyed almost unlimited freedom, hired armies of their own and led them to their private battles without the consent of the king. The sources of their power were not only their land and gold but also their lineages, which could often be traced back to royal ones. The film translation offers 'magnates' as an equivalent, which is again an example of normalization by generalization.

The representative of *królewięta* in the film, prince Wiśniowiecki, holds another title as well: *wojewoda*. At first voivodes were responsible for leading armies and passing judgements in their voivodeships but in the 17th century it was a title with few responsibilities, and yet one of high social status as voivodes had the right to be members of the Senate. The translator decided to use the procedure of covert cultural substitution and produced 'Governor'. As the rights and duties of a governor can vary greatly, depending on the country in which the term is used, it is an accurate choice; however, the unique administrative system is converted to generic western terms.

Since some events in the film are set between the death of one king and the election of another, at that time power is wielded by interim authorities. In the conversation with prince Wiśniowiecki, senator Kisiel presents the decision to grant Chmielnicki the rank of a hetman by saying: "Taka jest wola *Prymasa, Kanclerza i Senatu*", to stress that it is authorized by the senior authorities of the Commonwealth, including the Primate, who had the duties of the regent monarch, and the Chancellor, who was responsible for the foreign affairs and held the highest civic position in the Polish-Lithuanian Commonwealth. The translation is "Such is the will of the Senate". This is not inaccurate, as both the Primate and the Chancellor were also members of the Senate. The rendering is an example of normalization by generalization and even though it is not wrong from a historical point of view, it oversimplifies the situation and does not show the whole picture of the state's political scene.

The whole of parliament in the Polish-Lithuanian Commonwealth was referred to as *Sejm*. It consisted of three elements: representatives chosen by noblemen from the whole country, the Senate, which evolved from the Royal Council, and the king. The translator of the film chose the procedure of normalization by generalization but at the same time produced two renderings of the term. In one case, Gałązka-Salamon translated it as 'parliament', which properly reflects its functions, but loses the cultural uniqueness. In another scene, she translated it as 'nobles' consent', which is highly ambiguous: it is not specified whether the phrase should mean the consent of the nobles who are members of the parliament or the agreement of the whole of nobility.

There are also historical titles in use in the film. *Kniaź* is an old Slavic title of a local ruler, later used by rich landowners whose lineage could be traced to great Ruthenian and Lithuanian families, e.g. the Rurykowicz dynasty. The term was mostly used on Ruthenian lands, whereas in the rest of the Commonwealth such landowners were referred to as Princes. By the procedure of normalization by generalization, the translator unified these terms as 'Prince' and by doing so, eliminated the regional distinction.

When Prince Jeremi Wiśniowiecki speaks about the ancestors of Helena's family, he states: "Ród to stary, od *Rurykowiczów* się wywodzi". The Rurykowicz dynasty were a *kniaź* family who later became the rulers of the Duchy of Moscovia. As it has been explained before, all the families whose lineages could be traced back to families like Rurykowicze could be titled 'Princes', hence the titles of both Jeremi Wiśniowiecki and Helena Kurcewicz. Therefore, even though the difference in wealth between the two families was vast, they could be referred to with equal respect. In the translation, the procedure of normalization by generalization was used, producing "an old and noble family". However, given the double meaning of 'noble', the translation does not stress Helena's high status. She does belong to a noble family, but so does Rzędzian, Skrzetuski's servant. Therefore, the rendering seems deficient both in terms of cultural flavour and accuracy.

Family history is encapsulated in surnames and coats of arms. In the opening scene of the film Bohdan Chmielnicki is rescued by Skrzetuski. Before Skrzetuski agrees to shake his hand, Chmielnicki is forced to prove that he is a nobleman. He hides his true name, but he states his military rank and coat of arms: "Herbu Abdank z krzyżykiem". The part containing his coat of arms (called Abdank with a cross) is deleted in the translation. The probable reason for using this procedure is the lack of space in the subtitles, as Chmielnicki introduces himself in a rather lengthy manner. The Polish custom of treating a coat of arms like one's second surname is too much rooted in the unique Polish heraldic system, which could be confusing for a foreign viewer.

Podbipięta's family coat of arms (the aforementioned 'Hoodsnatcher') was won by his ancestor Stowejko in the Battle of Grunwald, the most famous battle for every Polish viewer. However, in Anglophone literature there is no consensus how the battle should be named, because the Teutonic Order referred to it as the Battle of Tannenberg. It is either because of that or due to the fact that to an English-speaking person neither of these names is familiar that the translator chose normalization. The name of the battle was simply replaced with the date '1410', which saves space as well as makes it easier to absorb by a viewer. However, removing the reference diminishes the role of the ancestor whom Longinus tries to imitate.

Practically in the next sentence, Longinus specifies it was none other than the famous king Władysław Jagiełło, the victor of the Battle of Grunwald and the architect of the first union between the Crown and the Grand Duchy of Lithuania, who granted his ancestor the title ("*Król Jagiełło* nadał mu herb"). The procedure of normalization by generalization produced "The king granted him the crest". From the term 'the king' alone, a non-Polish viewer would not know (and as a matter of fact would not care) who the great king was.

Also Chmielnicki is compared to a great predecessor of sorts: "Od czasów *hetmana Sahajdacznego* takiego wodza kozacy nie mieli". The above words, spoken by Prince Jeremi Wiśniowiecki, are meant as the highest praise of the leadership and tactical skills of Bohdan Chmielnicki. Piotr Konaszewicz Sahajdaczny is considered one of the greatest leaders of the Cossack armies and is famous for leading the Cossack forces in the Battle of Chocim. Along with Chmielnicki and a few others he is considered one of the greatest heroes of the Ukraine. However, to most modern Polish viewers and even more to English-speaking ones, he is not widely known, hence the procedure of deletion in the translation of this example: "It's been years since the Cossacks have had such a leader".

Material culture: weaponry

Problems in the translation of elements belonging to material culture involve not only rendering the names of the items but also their usage and appearance. Given the plot of the film, this category predominantly features terms for weaponry.

One of the most common elements is *szabla*. The sabre was a traditional weapon of both Polish noblemen and Cossacks. It replaced the long sword as a favourite weapon of Polish knights by the end of the 15th century due to the extensive contacts with Lithuania, Ruthenia and Hungary, and became an irreplaceable item for every nobleman. In order to translate the term, two different strategies have been used. Normalization by generalization resulted in the use of

'sword', with such elements as sabre-duels reduced to sword fighting, while deletion removed this crucial element of Eastern and Central European culture from
some scenes altogether. The term 'sabre' is used only three times throughout the
whole film: when Chmielnicki mentions the words of Władysław IV ("Haven't
you any guns and sabers?"), another time when one Cossack warns another
about Zagłoba ("Watch out, he's got his saber") and the last time when Zagłoba
taunts Bohun ("But don't be so eager to fight, as you have once fled from this
very saber").

Samopały is a term for primitive handheld firearms used in the 16th and
17th century on the lands of present-day Ukraine, Belarus and Russia. They were
muzzle-loaded and depended on an early version of a flintlock, which proved to
be defective. However, due to the simple design they were the most popular type
of firearm among the Cossacks, who used various models, depending on the
situation, short ones for personal usage and long ones for battle usage, against
cavalry, and as such they can be seen throughout the whole film in the hands
of Cossack soldiers. To translate the term, the procedure of normalization by
generalization was chosen and the end-product was the very generic term 'guns'.
With the disappearance of 'samopały', a contrast of technology between the more
modern army of the Commonwealth and the poorly equipped forces of Chmielnicki is lost as well.

Nahaj refers to a plaited leather whip with a short handle that was used by
Cossacks and other Ruthenians as a means of punishment or as a riding crop. This
unique cultural item came to Ruthenia through the Nogai Horde, from which it
also takes its name. Although in the film it can be seen on various occasions, it is
referred to only in the scene when Bohun threatens Helena. The translation procedure used in this case was, again, normalization by generalization ('whip').

Buława denotes a traditional and ceremonial mace of Polish-Lithuanian hetmans and military leaders of the Cossacks. It was a symbol of pride and power,
which was often incorporated into the coats of arms of the hetmans' families.
It consisted of a short handle and a round or pear-shaped ending which was
often decorated with gold, silver, and jewels. In the film it is visible in the hands
of Bohdan Chmielnicki, both when he uses it as a self-proclaimed hetman and
when senator Kisiel and a few other senators invest him with an official one. To
translate this unique cultural element the translator decided to use the procedure
of covert cultural substitution and produced 'baton', defined by *Oxford Dictionaries Online* as "a staff of office or authority, especially one carried by a field
marshal" (2011). Even though the element of authority is preserved, the shape of
the baton and its usage as a weapon is different, since apart from its usage in the
ancient times by the Romans, a baton, reintroduced in the Napoleonic era, is a

more modern invention than a 'buława'. A 'buława' is still functionally a weapon, whose uniqueness vanishes along with its cultural flavour and the domesticating rendering creates a slight anachronism.

Piernacz is a similar weapon and symbol of power, a small flanged mace used by Cossack officers and Polish magnates who had their lands in Ruthenia. Additionally, it constituted a proof of its wielder being an envoy, providing him with safe passage through enemy territory. In the film it is used both as a weapon, when Bohun nearly kills Rzędzian with it in his rage, and as a symbol of safe passage, used by Rzędzian to lead his friends to and from the witch's hiding place. 'Piernacz' is a smaller version of the aforementioned 'buława' and it was treated as such by the translator, who chose to once again use the procedure of covert cultural substitution and produced 'baton' as its equivalent. Unfortunately, it is the same term that was used previously to denote 'buława', which can create some confusion. A baton neither resembles a 'piernacz' nor does it serve as a symbol of an envoy.

Material culture: other items

Chleb z pajęczyną was known regionally by folk healers and medics and used as a universal treatment on open wounds. When these two ingredients are combined they create an antiseptic medicine that would increase the survival rate of those wounded in battle. The reason for its effectiveness was not discovered until the 20th century and the invention of penicillin out of the same mould that starts to grow on the combination of saliva, bread and cobwebs. In *With Fire and Sword* this form of treatment is used every time a person is wounded; however, in the translation of the film it was decided that the best procedure would be deletion.

In one of the first scenes of the film Zagłoba yells his order to a servant girl at an inn, demanding *trójniak*, a specific kind of mead, a regionally unique alcoholic beverage whose main ingredient is honey. It has been drunk in Poland along with beer since the middle ages. Meads have been traditionally segregated into different kinds on the basis of the ratio between honey and water into 'półtorak' (1:0,5 ratio), 'dwójniak' (1:1 ratio), 'trójniak' (1:2 ratio) and 'czwórniak' (1:3 ratio). The translation of this term is an example of normalization by generalization as the specific term is translated as 'mead'. The same term is used when the beverage is mentioned as 'miód'.

Apart from drinking mead, both noblemen and common people in the 17th century enjoyed drinking vodka. It was drunk in the Commonwealth almost as often as beer and definitely more often than wine due to the fact that it was relatively easy and cheap to produce. Due to its popularity there have been many names for it, depending on the region, the people who drank it and the times in which it was drunk, including *siwucha* and *gorzałka*. In the translation, the different names for this strong alcohol have been replaced with either 'vodka' or 'drink' due to the usage of the procedure of normalization by generalization.

Bandura denotes a traditional Ukrainian musical instrument similar to a lute, ranging from a medium, guitar-like size to a broad instrument possessing up to 60 strings. In the film, this folk instrument can be seen in the house of the Kurcewicz family, when Bohun is asked to sing a Cossack song. The translator used 'lute', which might be classified as normalization by generalization, because the 'bandura' belongs to the lute family; on the other hand, the design of this particular 'bandura' that Bohun uses bears similarity to the general look of a lute and thus the use of the term can be treated as a covert cultural substitution. However, a lute can be perceived as a symbol of poetry, of gentleness as well as of poetic soul, and introducing it as Bohun's attribute might influence his characterization.

Another item connected with music, *barabany* were traditional, massive kettledrums used both in music and in battle as signal tools in the Cossack armies as well as in Turkish and Polish ones (*tarabany*). In the film these elements appear twice: when Skrzetuski is transported to the Cossack encampment in the Sietch, and when they are used to fake attacks in the first battle between the Cossacks and the forces of the Commonwealth. The translator decided to utilize the procedure of normalization (generalization) and the end product was 'drums', which also have been used around the world to signal war.

"Masz konia *z rzędem*" is a proverbial phrase which means giving someone a great reward in exchange for completing a difficult task. However, in the film it has a literal meaning, as Rzędzian is rewarded with an actual horse along with an actual horse tack in exchange for gathering important information. The translated phrase uses the procedure of normalization by specification and features 'saddle'. It should be noted that even though a saddle is the most recognizable element of a tack, it is but a single element among many different ones, such as breastplates, brindles, halters, or reins. This procedure could have been used in order to make the situation easier to understand by replacing a specialized term ('horse tack') with the commonly known 'saddle', but at the same time such a rendering lowers the overall value of the reward, and the aspect of greed is an important one in the creation of the character of Rzędzian.

Hajdawery were wide, baggy Oriental trousers, popular among the Cossacks as well as other men in the Commonwealth. In the film, they can be seen on almost every Cossack, and they are mentioned by Zagłoba when he jokes about Bohun and his escape. The translator rendered this term as 'trousers', which is an example of the normalization (generalization) procedure.

Religious terms

Among cultural items used in the film whose translation could cause difficulties, there are three religious terms.

In the 17th century, the term *bisurman* referred to Muslims, especially those whose countries shared borders with the Polish-Lithuanian Commonwealth. In the film, this term appears when guests who are staying in the house of the Kurcewicz family propose a toast to the future war against the Ottoman Empire. The translator of the film chose the procedure of normalization (generalization) and produced 'infidels'. This might create an impression that the Cossacks are preparing for a holy war or a crusade against the Muslims, which is not the case in this situation. The aims of Cossacks in this war are supposed to be conquest and spoils of war, not spreading the Christian faith. Additionally, viewers might be puzzled when in further scenes the same Cossacks are in league with these very "infidels", showing no signs of any religious tension throughout the film.

In the scene following the kidnapping of Helena, Bohun compares her to an icon: "Jak obraz *w cerkwi*". Due to the fact that Bohun belongs to the Eastern Orthodox Church, he compares his beloved one to sacred paintings in Orthodox churches, ones to be looked at but not touched. The translator rendered this line as "like a church Madonna", with 'cerkiew', an Orthodox church, being reduced in the translation to a 'church'. Such normalization by generalization makes less visible the binary opposition between the Orthodox Cossacks and the Roman Catholic nobility, including Prince Jeremi Wiśniowiecki.

Enraged, Bohun then threatens to marry Helena by force: "Dziś jeszcze *popa* kazałbym za łeb przyprowadzić". This example also refers to the Eastern Orthodox Church. Gałązka-Salamon translated the term 'pop' as 'priest', using the procedure of normalization (generalization). Again, the difference between religions and parts of the Commonwealth is less visible. The form 'Orthodox priest' would take more space in the subtitles, make it more difficult to follow the fast speech of enraged Bohun, and would sound artificial in such a situation.

Miscellaneous terms

As can be inferred from the above examples, the dominant translation strategy tends towards domestication by normalization, which is well illustrated by two more examples.

"*Dziecina, Łacina i Pierzyna*" are the derisive nicknames of the three commanders appointed after both hetmans of the Crown had been captured in the battle of Korsuń in 1648. 'Dziecina' (Child) refers to Aleksander Koniecpolski, who was only twenty-eight at that time, 'Łacina' (Latin) refers to Mikołaj

Ostroróg, an erudite who lacked practical experience, and 'Pierzyna' (Feather Quilt) refers to Władysław Dominik Zasławski, notorious for his sloth. The procedure for translating this mocking rhyme can be classified as normalization by generalization bordering on deletion because the whole line is removed and replaced with 'three weaklings'.

"Chcesz *pala posmakować*?" is a threat uttered by Helena's mother towards Bohun in order to force him into obedience and persuade him not to seek a fight with Skrzetuski. It refers to the punishment of impalement, which was often chosen in Eastern Europe for those who were sentenced to death, especially members of the lower classes. Gałązka-Salamon decided to translate this example as "Do you want to be slain?", which could be interpreted as "being killed in the fight with that nobleman" rather than "being executed for a serious crime in a horrible and degrading way". It is an example of normalization by generalization and the threat is preserved; however, the choice is quite puzzling given that the very method of execution is illustrated in a subsequent scene.

Conclusions

Due to the application of translation procedures reflecting a domesticating strategy, the text gained "fluency", allowing a viewer who is not familiar with the culture of the 17th century Commonwealth to enjoy the film without any disturbing occurrences of unfamiliar elements. Moreover, space in the subtitles was saved and the number of words per second was kept on a level acceptable for the viewers. On the other hand, the general feeling of cultural flavour and uniqueness was lost due to the translator's attempts to avoid exoticism. Paradoxically, some examples prove that going to great lengths with domestication procedures might cause the viewer to get confused too, and lead to misunderstandings of a more serious kind. Finally, particular applications of domestication strategies led to vital changes in the representation of different cultures existing and fighting with each other in the film.

References

Aixela, Javier Franco. 1996. "Culture-specific items in translation", in Roman Alvarez and M. Carmen-Africa Vidal (eds.) *Translation, power, subversion*, 52–78.

Alvarez, Roman and M. Carmen-Africa Vidal (eds.) 1996. *Translation, power, subversion*. Clevedon-Bristol-Adelaide: Multilingual Matters Ltd.

Hoffman, Jerzy (dir.) 1999. *Ogniem i mieczem*. DVD edition. Warszawa: ITI Cinema.

Kwieciński, Piotr. 2001. *Disturbing Strangeness. Foreignization and domestication in translation procedures in the context of cultural asymmetry.* Toruń: Wydawnictwo Edytor.

Oxford Dictionaries Online. 2011. http://oxforddictionaries.com, DOA April 13, 2011.

Venuti, Lawrence. 1995. *The translator's invisibility. A history of translation.* London-New York: Routledge.

Natalia Grabowska

From the Orient Westwards. Cultural items in two English translations of *Sonety krymskie* by Adam Mickiewicz

The present article discusses the translation of culture-specific items in *Sonety krymskie* by Adam Mickiewicz. *Sonety krymskie* is a cycle of eighteen sonnets, published in 1826, constituting an account of the poet's journey to Crimea. An expression of reflections and impressions rather than an authentic description of the chronological course of the journey (Kleiner 1995: 581), the cycle is considered as one of the most recognizable works in Polish poetry.

The paper analyses translations of *Sonety krymskie* by Edna Worthley Underwood (published in 1917) and Michał J. Mikoś (published in 1998). The translations above were selected for the study as they are the most popular and cover the greatest number of sonnets: Underwood translated sixteen sonnets, whereas Mikoś rendered the whole cycle of eighteen poems.

The analysis is primarily based on the division of cultural items by Peter Newmark (1988), and a classification of procedures reflecting domesticating and foreignising approach by Piotr Kwieciński (2001).

The article initially focuses on the portrayal of the Orient in *Sonety krymskie* and provides an explanation of selected culture-specific items from the cycle. Subsequently, it compares the translation of cultural items by Underwood and Mikoś, which is followed by conclusions.

Orientalism in *Sonety krymskie*

Orientalism is one of the most important issues in the study of *Sonety krymskie*, and there have been many attempts to define and evaluate the Oriental character of the sonnets. According to Edward Said's definition, Orientalism is "a distribution of geopolitical awareness into aesthetic, scholarly, economic, sociological, historical and philosophical texts [...] It *is*, rather than expresses, a certain will or intention to understand, in some cases to control, manipulate, even incorporate, what is manifestly different world" (Said 1978: 12 in Ashcroft and Griffiths 2009).

In *Sonety krymskie*, Mickiewicz introduced changes to the content and style of the cycle in order to increase the poems' Oriental character (Kwaśny 1966: 419). When analysing autographs by Mickiewicz, Kwaśny distinguished two phases in the creation of the cycle: the preliminary description, insignificantly marked by Eastern elements, and the later introduction of additional exotic terms and stylistic devices typical for the Oriental style. For instance, the revised version of verses 3 and 4 from the sonnet "Widok gór ze stepów Kozłowa" introduces Oriental terms and stylisation to enhance the exotic character of the sonnet: *Divs* appear in place of *people* and *stars* are turned into *the caravan of stars*. (Kwaśny 1966: 419). Generally, Kwaśny indicates that Mickiewicz decided to change the style into a more Oriental one that features the frequent use of hyperbole (425). Moreover, the poet modified certain equivalents of Arabic proper names to make them sound more exotic. For example, in the sonnet "Droga nad przepaścią w Czufut Kale", the standard Polish spelling of Cairo (*Kair*) was modified by Mickiewicz into *Al-Kair*, and finally into *Al-Kahir* (420–421).

The religion of Islam is also treated as an exotic feature. Kleiner claims that the character of Mirza is introduced not only to explain the Oriental culture to the pilgrim, as his monologues serve primarily to introduce religious context into the sonnets. Moreover, by dint of the presence of Mirza, the Oriental style of the cycle is justified and does not appear artificial. (1995: 574) The implementation of the religious context enabled further introduction of both mythological and fairy-tale contexts to *Sonety krymskie*. (1995: 575, 578)

Attitude towards the Oriental culture

In the interpretations used for the present study, the speaker in *Sonety krymskie* is frequently defined as a pilgrim or a poet who comes to an unknown land. The poet portrays Crimea by means of associations, metaphorical language and comparisons (Opacki 1972: 17), as he gradually acquires knowledge about the land from Mirza, a character who functions as a representative of the East and explains the foreign culture to the pilgrim (Kalinowska-Blackwood 1998: 431). Still, it should be indicated the pilgrim's feeling of disorientation can be understood also in a metaphorical sense. Opacki indicates that it is not only Crimea that is unfamiliar for the pilgrim, but also his own mind. (Opacki 1972: 18)

The attitude of the pilgrim towards Mirza as a representative of the Oriental culture was analysed by Izabela Kalinowska-Blackwood, who relates to Edward Said's theory of Orientalism and attempts to verify the extent to which *Sonety krymskie* mirror the common pattern by which Europeans used to portray the Orient. She observes that the pilgrim considers Mirza as "independent and different", which makes it possible for him to start a dialogue and obtain help. The difference between the two does not prevent the creation of a relationship. The pilgrim is defined as empathetic and open for the distinctness of the Oriental culture. (1998: 431–432) Kalinkowska-Blackwood claims that *Sonety krymskie,* with regard to their artistic formation and the political situation in the days of their publication, do not imitate Western hegemonic ideas of the Orient, but show that dialogue is possible between the two cultures (1998: 439).

Given the subsequent case study on the renderings of *Sonety krymskie,* the following conclusions can be drawn: the above-mentioned critics agree that the descriptions in the cycle present a vision of reality that is limited to the experience and knowledge of the pilgrim, who gradually becomes familiar with the foreign culture. The presentation of Crimea is subjective and constitutes a parallel to the emotional state of the speaker. Oriental terms for exotic places and objects provide information about the foreign land but primarily create the exotic character of the cycle. Although the presentation of Crimea is considered truthful and consistent with the reality of those days in many respects, it should be indicated that the main focus of the sonnets was to create a sense of astonishment in readers, and this aesthetic function predominated over the other ones.

Cultural items and proper names in the source text

As described before, Mickiewicz introduced a significant number of cultural elements into the sonnets. Terms for Oriental places, persons, customs, fauna and flora chiefly contribute to the exotic character of the sonnets. In the present paper these elements are classified on the basis on Newmark's (1988) division, and include proper names and non-institutional culture-specific items. The former category is restricted to geographical names for places mentioned in the source text: *Ajudah, Ałuszta, Al-Kahir, Bajdary, Bakczysaraj, Bałakława, Carogród, Czufut-Kale, Czatyrdah, Dniestr, Kikineis, Krym, Litwa, Sahir, stepy Akermańskie, stepy Kozłowa,* and *Tarkankut* (17 items altogether). Among the remaining 48 items, the following subcategories can be distinguished:

1) fauna and flora: terms for animals and plants (*ananasy, cyprys, morwy, ostrowy burzanu, powój, słowiki Bajdaru, szarańcza*);
2) religious terms: terms for transcendental beings, people, places, objects and concepts connected with Islam and Christianity (*Allach, całun, chalif, chylat, Diwy, dżamid, dywan Eblisa, Gabryjel, Giaur, głoski Balsazara, izan, kurhan, minaret, menar, Muślimin, pieśni namaza, Prorok, róże edeńskie, szatan, turban*);
3) military terms, official titles and symbols of power (*basze, buńczuk, drogman, Farys, Giraje, janczary, Mirza, padyszach*);
4) other items (*ateńskie ozdoby, baldachim, fontanna haremu, góra-ptak, harem, hrabina Potocka, Italczyk, mekkański przybylec, Mongołowie, stepy, wschodnia odaliska*).

Mickiewicz enclosed a total of 22 explanations for proper names and cultural items in the volume, referring to *Collectanea z dziejów tureckich rzeczy do historii polskiej służących* by Józef Sękowski. The present discussion will capitalise on the description provided by Mickiewicz, but also on the definitions from *Słownik języka polskiego PWN* (SJP) and *Słownik wyrazów obcych PWN* (SWO). The definitions of particularly ambiguous and controversial terms will be presented on the basis of *Z Mickiewiczem na Krymie* by Wacław Kubacki and *Świat sonetów krymskich* by Stanisław Makowski. The two publications, together with *Mickiewicz* by Juliusz Kleiner, were the only materials among the references used in this work that included definitions for the cultural items in *Sonety krymskie*; however, the explanations presented in the first two sources were considerably more detailed. Several biological terms are explained on the basis of *Encyklopedia powszechna PWN*.

A significant number of geographical names (9 out of 17) appear in the titles of the sonnets. Mickiewicz defined *Chatyrdah* as the highest peak in the Crimean mountains (1967: 42). *Bakczysaraj*, according to his explanation, is a former capital of the rulers of Crimea (1967: 43), and *Salhir* – a river with its spring in Chatyrdah (1967: 46). The eponymous Ajudah from which the poet observed and described the sea is often misinterpreted as a mountain, while Makowski explains that what Mickiewicz named *Ajudah* in the sonnet is merely a boulder located near the coast. (1969: 157–160) The term *Carogród*, according to *Encyklopedia powszechna* (1987: 269), is a name for Istanbul used among southern and eastern Slavs from the 9th to the 11th century.

Generally, Kleiner claims that by his use of geographical names Mickiewicz primarily attempts to reflect the atmosphere of the places he mentions in *Sonety krymskie*, not necessarily to present them in a realistic way (1995: 581). Łucja Szewczyk distinguishes three major functions of the proper names used in *Sonety krymskie*: locative, allusive and poetic. The names for geographical places locate the created reality in a concrete space. The allusive function, on the other hand, is connected with placing the text in the historical and cultural reality, as the proper names create associations with well-known figures or motives. The poetic function consists in the use of proper names within stylistic devices. Moreover, the names' sound and spelling themselves contribute to the exotic, Oriental character of the sonnets. (Szewczyk 1994: 110–112)

The most numerous group of cultural elements in the sonnets is formed by religious terms. Most of these terms describe persons, places and objects connected with Islam. Nouns such as *namaz*, *izan* or *dżamid* introduce the reader into the sphere of Islamic culture. Mickiewicz defines *namaz* as a kind of prayer said by Muslims, *izan* as convoking people for a prayer, and *dżamid* as a mosque

(1967: 43, 44). Nonetheless, Kubacki perceives Mickiewicz's definition for the last term as misleading. He refers to *Dziennik podróży do Turcji* by Edward Raczyński and presents the distinction between *meczet* – a chapel (*kaplica*) and *dżamid* – a larger structure where not only prayers, but also sermons may be held (Kubacki 1977: 230). A *minaret* or *menar* is a steeple turret with a gallery from which the sound of *izan* travels (Mickiewicz 1967: 43). Mickiewicz also explains that *Diwy* in Persian mythology were mean genii forced by angels to leave the Earth and now inhabiting the end of the world (1967: 42). *Eblis* is defined as an Islamic equivalent of satan (1967: 43). *Giaur* is a term that Muslims use in reference to Christians (1967: 45). *Słownik języka polskiego* (2005: 393) defines *kurhan* as a large historical grave or a tumulus celebrating a person or event. *Turban* mentioned in the sonnet "Mogiły haremu", according to Mickiewicz, is a reference to stone turbans placed above graves (Mickiewicz 1967: 45). The sonnets also feature Biblical terms, such as *szatan, róże edeńskie* or *głoski Balsazara*. The last expression, used in the sonnet "Bakczysaraj", is an allusion to the fifth part of the Prophecy of Daniel about the destruction of Belshazzar's kingdom, which Mickiewicz quotes in his explanation of the expression (Mickiewicz: 1967: 43).

Most of the terms for fauna and flora do not appear difficult; however, several items should be explained. The author defines *burzan* as large bushes that bloom in summer (Mickiewicz 1967: 42). Makowski claims that the most accurate definition for this term was the one given by Kazimierz Wyka in *Wielka encyklopedia ilustrowana*, where *burzan* means various steppe or field weeds, especially thistles. (*Słownik języka polskiego* 2005: 621) However, Kubacki proposes a different explanation of *burzan* as various weeds, without the possibility to determine particular species or geographical regions (1977: 252).

Another group of the cultural items in *Sonety krymskie* consists of official titles and military terms. *Girej*, according to Makowski, is the title of the last ruler in Crimea (1969: 64). *Mirza*, the character who explains Oriental culture to the pilgrim, can be defined as a title in the Far East and the Middle East. When the term *mirza* is used after a name, it indicates a duke; when it is used before it, it indicates a dignitary and erudite (SWO 2002: 728). *Kalif* (contemporary, modernised spelling of Mickiewicz's *chalif*) is a Muslim leader, both religious and political one (2002: 512). *Drogman* can be defined as a guide (Kleiner 1995: 574). *Padyszach* is, following Mickiewicz, a Turkish sultan (1967: 45). Another term, *janczary* (janissaries), is defined in *Słownik języka polskiego* as denoting Christian captives forced to serve in the Turkish infantry (2005: 290). *Buńczuk* means a part of a horse's tail attached to a pole weapon – a symbol used by Turkish and Polish military commanders (2005: 72). *Farys*, as defined by Mickiewicz, is an Arab knight (1967: 44). *Basze*, according to *Słownik wyrazów obcych,* are Turkish civil or military dignitaries (2002: 114). The term *góra-ptak* from the category of miscellaneous items is explained by the poet as a motif deriving from *One Thousand and One Nights*, referring to the bird Simurg of Persian mythology, characterised as strong and of immense size. (Mickiewicz 1967: 46–47)

Translation of cultural items and proper names in *Sonety krymskie*

As visible above, the choice of the cultural elements, their number and the perspective from which they are presented are undoubtedly important and should be taken into consideration when translating *Sonety krymskie*.

This paper will now examine the cycle of eighteen sonnets translated by Mikoś and the cycle of sixteen sonnets translated by Underwood (sonnets III and IV, "Burza" and "Żegluga", were not rendered by the latter translator). In the analysis, renderings of all the culture-specific items from the source texts were compared with their equivalents in the target text, and the procedures used by the two translators were determined. The classification of procedures was based on the model proposed by Kwieciński (2001).

The aim of the research was to determine which strategy of translating cultural items was adopted the most frequently by a particular translator. I expected that Edna Underwood, a poet translator with a background in the target culture, would mostly rely on domestication in order to make the text more understandable for the target audience, whereas the Polish translator would be more likely to employ foreignisation in order to emphasise the cultural elements introduced by Mickiewicz. Also, his introduction of explanations of the terms to his rendition of the cycle could suggest a tendency to use foreignisation.

The study of the translation of proper names and cultural items in *Sonety krymskie* is based on the analysis of 65 items. As indicated before, the items are classified according to Newmark's categorisation of proper names and cultural terms, and represent two categories: proper names (17 items), and non-institutional cultural terms (48 items). The second group is further divided into four subcategories: fauna and flora, religious terms, official titles and military terms, and a subcategory called *other*. The items are presented in tables together with the context in which they appear. They are also accompanied by their translations and the name of the procedure used by a given translator. The most interesting examples from each category are discussed below the respective tables.

Still, it should be indicated that some of the items may appear ambiguous, and therefore in several instances it was difficult to categorise them and to definitely label the procedures used by the translators.

It is also essential to note that the explanations of the cultural items provided by Mickiewicz in the original volume of *Sonety krymskie* were omitted in the rendering by Underwood, who also wrote additional fourteen definitions of cultural items of her own.

Table 1: Geographical names

Cultural item	Underwood	Procedure	Mikoś	Procedure
Ajudah	Juda's cliff	calque	Ajudah	borrowing + normalization, external gloss
Ałuszta	Aluszta	borrowing, adapted importation	Aluszta	borrowing, adapted importation + normalization, external gloss
Al-Kahir	–	deletion	Cairo	recognised exoticism + normalization, external gloss
Bajdary	Baydary	borrowing, adapted importation	Baydary	borrowing, adapted importation
Bakczysaraj	Baktschi Serai	borrowing, adapted importation	Bakhchisaray	recognised exoticism, recognised equivalent
Bałakława	Balaclava	borrowing, adapted importation	Balaklava	borrowing, adapted importation
Dniestr	Dneister	borrowing, adapted importation	Dniester	recognised exoticism, recognised equivalent + normalization, external gloss
Carogród	pagan cities	normalization	Stamboul	substitution for a different source culture element
Czatyrdah	Tschatir Dagh	borrowing, adapted importation	Chatyr Dag	recognised equivalent
Czufut-Kale	Tschufut-Kale	borrowing, adapted importation	Chufut-Kale	borrowing, adapted importation

Cultural item	Underwood	Procedure	Mikoś	Procedure
Kikineis	–	deletion	Kikineiz	borrowing, adapted importation + normalization, external gloss
Krym	Crimean land	recognised exoticism + normalization, internal gloss	Crimea	recognized exoticism, recognised equivalent
Litwa	home land	normalization	Lithuania	calque
Salhir	–	deletion	Salhir	borrowing
stepy Akermańskie	Ackerman Steppe	borrowing, adapted importation	Akkerman steppes	recognised exoticism, recognised equivalent
stepy Kozłowa	the Kezlov Steppe	borrowing, adapted importation	the Kozlov Steppes	recognised exoticism + normalization, external gloss
Tarkankut	–	deletion	Tarkankut	borrowing, importation + normalization, external gloss

The name *Ajudah* occurs twice in *Sonety krymskie*. Once it is used in the title of the last sonnet in the cycle, and it also appears in the first verse of this sonnet: "Lubię poglądać wsparty na Judahu skale…" The sentence might have influenced the translation of *Ajudah* into *Juda's cliff* by Underwood; however, as it was indicated in the explanations of cultural items and proper names from the source text, Ajudah is not actually a mountain or a cliff, but merely a boulder. Mikoś did not introduce any semantic extension in the title. He merely borrowed the source item and placed the explanation of the term in a footnote. In the first verse, he avoided the above-mentioned inaccuracy by introducing a metaphorical expression, *on Ajudah's face*.

The original name for the city of Al-Kahir in Arabic is Al-Qāhirah, which means the Victorious (*Encyclopaedia Britannica*). Thus, in the source text this word is an adapted borrowing from Arabic. The translation by Mikoś does not reflect the Arabic version, but the recognized English translation of this item.

The first translation of *Bakczysaraj* is one of the multiple examples which show the major procedure used by Underwood in translating geographical names. Whereas Mikoś used existing English equivalents for the above names,

Underwood borrowed the names and adapted their spelling to the target language.

As it was indicated before, *Carogród*, according to *Encyklopedia Powszechna* (1987: 269), is the name for the city now called Istanbul, used by southern and eastern Slavs when they considered it their religious and cultural centre. Thus, one may infer that the term used by Mikoś does not refer to the past city, as in the source text, but to the city in Turkey contemporary to the author.

Whereas Mikoś used an existing English equivalent for *Litwa* (Lithuania), Underwood introduced the phrase *home land*, which transfers the emotional value.

Table 2: Flora and fauna

Cultural item	Context	Underwood	Procedure	Mikoś	Procedure
ananasy	I weselszy deptałem twoje trzęsawice/ Niż rubinowe morwy, złote ananasy	–	Deletion	pineapple plants	recognised exoticism, recognised equivalent + normalization, internal gloss
cyprys	Tu cień pada z menaru i wierzchu cyprysa	cypress	recognised exoticism	cypress tree	recognised exoticism, recognised equivalent + normalization, internal gloss
morwy	I weselszy deptałem twoje trzęsawice/ Niż rubinowe morwy, złote ananasy	–	deletion	–	deletion
ostrowy burzanu	…śród kwiatów powodzi/ omijam koralowe ostrowy burzanu	blossom-isles	Mutation	isles of thistledown	Calque
powój	Skroś okien różnofarbnych powoju roślina/ Wdzierając się na głuche ściany i sklepienia…	ivy	substitution for a different element	bindweed	recognised exoticism, recognised equivalent
słowiki Bajdaru	Litwo! piały mi wdzięczniej twe szumiące lasy/ Niż słowiki Bajdaru	–	deletion	Baydary nightingales	Calque

Cultural item	Context	Underwood	Procedure	Mikoś	Procedure
szarańcza	Sofy, trony potęgi (...)/ Przeskakuje szarańcza, obwija gadzina	cricket	substitution for a different element	locust	recognised exoticism, recognised equivalent
szarańcza	Dalej szarańcza ciągnie swój całun skrzydlaty	cicadas	substitution for a different element	locust	recognised exoticism, recognised equivalent
szarańcza	Czy szarańcza plon zetnie, czy giaur pali domy	–	deletion	locust	recognised exoticism, recognised equivalent

In both translations the item *morwy* was omitted; however, the translators introduced new culture-specific items, or retained other culture-specific items from the stanza in which this verse occurs. This could be explained by the fact that, as Makowski indicated in his interpretation of *Sonety krymskie* (1969: 110–112), the cultural items present in the above verse were used merely to introduce exoticism and to create contrast between the pilgrim's homeland and Crimea. Furthermore, Sawrymowicz (1968: 10) explains that pineapple could never be found in Crimea, and mulberry becomes ruby-coloured in June, whereas Mickiewicz was in Crimea from late August to late September. Thus, accuracy in translation does not appear essential in this case.

Bindweed is defined as a wild plant that wraps itself around other plants when growing (*Cambridge Dictionary*), which also characterises the plant from the source text. *Ivy* is further defined as a plant that often grows up buildings or trees, so it would correspond to the Polish term *bluszcz*. Thus, the procedure employed by Underwood is classified as a substitution for a different item.

The verses in which *szarańcza* is mentioned describe a palace in ruins, and the description of insects and animals living inside emphasises its decline. *Locust*, the direct translation by Mikoś, denotes an insect that flies in large swarms and destroys plants; it also retains the Biblical connotations. *Cricket*, used by Underwood (substitution for a different element) adds a sound effect to the verse. In another place, Underwood's translation of this item also includes a sound effect, as *cicadas* are insects making characteristic high sounds. (*Cambridge Dictionary*)

Table 3: Religious terms

Cultural item	Context	Underwood	Procedure	Mikoś	Procedure
Allach	Tam? Czy Allach postawił ścianą morze lodu?	Great Allah	borrowing	Allah	borrowing
całun	Dalej szarańcza ciągnie swój całun skrzydlaty	–	deletion	veil	normalization
chalif	las... sypie z majowego włosa, / Jak z różańca chalifów, rubin i granaty	calif	borrowing, adapted importation	caliph	recognized exoticism
chylat	Już góra z piersi mgliste otrząsa chylaty	mist-veil	coinage	mantles	normalization, generalization
Diwy	Czy Diwy z ćwierci lądu dźwignęli te mury,/ Aby gwiazd karawanę nie puszczać ze wschodu?	demons	normalization, generalization	Divs	borrowing, adapted importation
dżamid	Rozchodzą się z dżamidów pobożni mieszkańce	mosque	normalization	mosque	normalization
dywan Eblisa	Jak szatany siedzące w dywanie Eblisa	–	deletion	council of Eblis	calque
Gabryjel	Siedzisz sobie pod bramą niebios, jak wysoki/ Gabryjel	Gabriel	recognised exoticism	Gabriel	recognised exoticism
Giaur	Czy sarańcza płot zetnie, czy giaur pali domy – / Czatyrdachu, ty zawsze głuchy, nieruchomy	giaour	recognised exoticism	Giaour	recognised exoticism
głoski Balsazara	Zajmuje dzieło ludzi w imię przyrodzenia/ I pisze Balsazara głoskami >>RUINA<<	Belshazzar-like curse	recognised exoticism + normalization, internal gloss	Balthazar's letters	recognised exoticism + normalization, external gloss

Cultural item	Context	Underwood	Procedure	Mikoś	Procedure
Izan	Odgłos izanu w cichym gubi się wieczorze	Muezzin	substitution for a different source culture element	prayer	normalization, generalization
kurhan	Już mrok zapada, nigdzie drogi ni kurhanu	–	deletion	kurgan	borrowing, adapted importation + normalization, external gloss
minaret	O minarecie świata!.../ Ty, nad skały poziomu uciekłszy w obłoki, / Siedzisz sobie pod bramą niebios...	minaret	borrowing, importation	minaret	borrowing, importation
menar	Tu cień pada z menaru	–	deletion	menar	borrowing
Muślimin	Drżąc muślimin całuje stopy twej opoki, / ...wielki Chatyrdachu!	Mussulman	borrowing, adapted importation	Muslims	recognised exoticism, recognised equivalent
pieśni namaza	I mekkański przybylec nucił pieśń namaza	–	deletion	songs of prayers	normalization, generalization
Prorok	Teraz grób wasz spojrzenie cudzoziemca plami,/ Pozwalam mu, – darujesz, o wielki Proroku!	Allah	substitution for a different source-text element	Prophet	recognised exoticism, recognised equivalent + external gloss
róże edeńskie	O wy, róże edeńskie! U czystości stoku/ Odkwiknęły dni wasze pod wstydu liściami	roses of this paradise of old	normalization	roses of Eden	calque
szatan	Dalej czernią się kołem olbrzymy granitu,/ Jak szatany siedzące w dywanie Eblisa	Lucifer	substitution for a different element	fiend	normalization, generalization
turban	Nad nimi turban zimny błyszczy śród ogrodu	turban	recent borrowing	turban	recent borrowing

The addition of the adjective *great* in Underwood's rendering of *Allach* does not introduce an explanation (gloss) or a new meaning (semantic extension), but is considered to be implemented for aesthetic effect.

In the case of *chalif*, Mikoś used a target culture equivalent for the term, whereas Underwood merely adapted the source text item to the English spelling.

In Mikoś's translation the culture-specific item *chylat* is replaced by a common noun, therefore the procedure is classified as normalization, since *mantle* is simply a layer that covers something (*Cambridge Dictionary*). Underwood introduced a neologism, *mist-veil*, with *veil* being much more specific (a fragment of material that covers a woman's head or face) (*Cambridge Dictionary*). The procedure she employed is defined as coinage.

As it was explained before, *głoski Balsazara* is an allusion to a Biblical story, the content of which justifies the use of the word *curse* in Underwood's translation. Underwood's spelling of the name responds to the one used in King James Version of the Bible.

Underwood substituted *izan*, a term for prayer, with a different element, although still characteristic for the culture in question, since a *muezzin* is an official who calls Muslims to prayer (*Encyclopaedia Britannica*). Mikoś, on the other hand, used a common noun instead of the culture-specific item, so the procedure is defined as normalization.

Both translators preserved the term *minaret*. However, Sawrymowicz (1968: 12) indicates that the use of the term in reference to Czatyrdach is another inaccuracy, as the comparison suggests a spire-like shape of the mountain, whereas in reality it is a massive mountain of a roughly trapezoid shape.

Mikoś included an explanation of the term *Prorok* as referring to prophet Muhammad. Underwood, on the other hand, substituted the term for *Allah*, a different culture-specific element.

Table 4: *Official titles and military terms*

Cultural item	Context	Underwood	Procedure	Mikoś	Procedure
basze	Zmiatane czołem baszów ganki i przedsienia	–	deletion	pashas	recognised exoticism
buńczuk	Nad nimi turban zimny błyszczy śród ogrodu, / Jak buńczuk wojska cieniów	banner	normalization, generalization	ensign	normalization, generalization + external gloss
drogman	Między światem i niebem, jak drogman stworzenia	–	deletion	the world you explain	normalization
Farys	Budzi się błyskawica i pędem Farysa/ Przelatuje...	Arab steed	substitution for a different element	farys	recent borrowing + normalization, external gloss
Giraje	Jeszcze wielka, już pusta Girajów dziedzina!	the Tartar Khan	recognised exoticism	Gireys	borrowing, adapted importation
janczary	Ciemny las twoim płaszczem, a janczary strachu/ Twój turban z chmur haftują błyskawic potoki	–	deletion	janissaries	recognised exoticism
Mirza	Mirzo, a ja spojrzałem! Przez świata szczeliny...	Mirza	recognised exoticism, recognised equivalent	Mirza	recognised exoticism, recognised equivalent
padyszach	O minarecie świata! o gór Padyszachu! / Ty, nad skały poziomu uciekłszy w obłoki, / Siedzisz sobie pod bramą niebios	–	deletion	padishah	borrowing, adapted importation

Instead of rendering the cultural item *drogman* directly, Mikoś explains its function, employing the procedure of normalization.

Farys was defined by Mickiewicz as a knight or horseman (1967: 44). Underwood substituted the term for a different item associated with Oriental culture.

Girej is a proper name constituting the title of the last ruler in Crimea, and *Khan* is a term that denotes a title of a ruler in Turkish and Mongolian languages. Thus, the procedure used by Underwood is classified as a recognised exoticism.

Table 5: Other items

Cultural item	Context	Underwood	Procedure	Mikoś	Procedure
ateńskie ozdoby	Tu Grek dłutował w murach ateńskie ozdoby	columned marble	normalization	Athenian ornaments	calque
Baldachim	Motyle różnofarbne, niby tęczy kosa,/ Baldachimem z brylantów okryły niebiosa;	band (of butterflies)	normalization, generalization	shade	normalization, generalization
fontanna haremu	W środku sali wycięte z marmuru naczynie/To fontanna haremu: dotąd stoi cało,/I perłowe łzy sącząc woła przez pustynie	the fountain of the harem	Calque	the harem fountain	calque
góra-ptak	...wśród fali zda się, że ptak-góra, / Piorunem zastrzelony, swe masztowe pióra/ Roztoczył kręgiem, szerszym niż tęczy półkole	giant bird divine	normalization, internal gloss	mountain-bird	calque
Harem	Błyszczą w haremie niebios wieczne gwiazd kagańce	Harem	recent borrowing	harem	recent borrowing
Italczyk	Stąd Italczyk Mongołom narzucał żelaza	Latin	superordinate, substitution for another SC element	Italian	recognized exoticism, recognized equivalent

Cultural item	Context	Underwood	Procedure	Mikoś	Procedure
mekkański przybylec	mekkański przybylec nucił pieśń namaza	Mussulmans	normalization, repacking	settler from Mecca	calque
Mongołowie	Stąd Italczyk Mongołom narzucał żelaza	Mongol horde	recognised exoticism + internal gloss	Mongol	recognised exoticism
Stepy	Stepy Akermańskie (in the title)	Steppes	recognised exoticism, recognised equivalent	steppes	recognised exoticism, recognised equivalent
wschodnia odaliska	Nocy wschodnia! ty na kształt wschodniej odaliski	odalisque	recognized exoticism	odalisque	recognized exoticism + external gloss
Potocka	grób Potockiej (in the title)	Countess Potocka	borrowing + normalization, internal gloss	Potocki	borrowing, adapted importation

Conclusion

The study concerning the translation of culture-specific items in *Sonety krymskie* appears to confirm the previous expectations that Michał J. Mikoś would attempt to preserve the cultural elements from the source text to a significantly greater extent than Edna Underwood, who frequently domesticated culture-specific items. The rendering of particular cultural items can be summarised as follows.

Geographical names were translated by Underwood mainly by the use of borrowing; however, the terms were adapted to the spelling of the target language. Mikoś used the existing official translations of the terms or employed the procedure of borrowing. However, he frequently gave explanations of selected terms in the footnotes, and included the footnotes provided by Mickiewicz in the source text.

Terms for fauna and flora were mainly translated by Underwood with the use of deletion, and by Mikoś with the use of recognised exoticism. Mikoś's translation of these terms is accurate and the terms correspond to the names of the species from the source text. Underwood, on the other hand, frequently omitted the terms or substituted them for other items, denoting different varieties or species. It appears that when translating fauna and flora, Underwood focused more on the aesthetic function of the sonnets than on the accuracy of translating particular terms.

Another group of cultural items that differed in the two translations are religious terms. This is one of the only two problem areas in which Underwood used foreignisation more often that domestication. This could be explained by the fact that these terms introduce a religious context that is essential for the culture of the East. Mikoś rendered religious terms by the use of various procedures, such as borrowing, recognised equivalents or normalization.

In Underwood's rendering of official titles and military terms, the procedure of deletion was also frequently employed. While Mikoś used multiple procedures such as calque, normalization and borrowing, Underwood often omitted official titles and military terms.

While rendering culture-specific items from the final, miscellaneous category, Underwood mostly used normalization, whereas Mikoś mainly employed calques and recognised exoticisms.

It can be assumed that Mikoś took the approach of foreignisation much more frequently than domestication to maintain most of the culture-specific items introduced by Mickiewicz, whereas Underwood frequently used domestication to make the cultural items more understandable for the target audience. Moreover, although domesticating and foreignising procedures were used by Underwood with almost the same frequency, she used domestication much more often than Mikoś, who applied this approach only in several instances. Underwood used foreignisation only when it appeared especially necessary, as in the rendering of geographical names or religious terms constituting an important element of the culture of the East.

References

Primary sources

Ashcroft, Bill and Gareth Griffiths. 2009. *Post-colonial studies. The key concepts.* London: Routledge.

Cambridge Advanced Learner's Dictionary. 2008. Cambridge: Cambridge University Press.

Encyclopaedia Britannica Online. Encyclopaedia Britannica. 2011. http://www.britannica.com, DOA May 12, 2011

Encyklopedia powszechna PWN. 2nd edition. 1987. Warszawa: Państwowe Wydawnictwo Naukowe.

Kalinkowska-Blackwood, Izabela. 1998. "The dialogue between East and West in the Crimean Sonnets", *The Polish Review* 43.4, 29–439.

Kleiner, Juliusz. 1995. *Mickiewicz,* vol. 1. Lublin: Wydawnictwo Towarzystwa Naukowego KUL.

Kubacki, Wacław. 1977. *Z Mickiewiczem na Krymie.* Warszawa: Państwowy Instytut Wydawniczy.

Kwaśny, Marcin. "Jak powstała szata orientalna Sonetów krymskich", in Marek Piechota (ed.) *Adam Mickiewicz. Materiały Śląskiej Sesji Mickiewiczowskiej Wyższej Szkoły Pedagogicznej, Katowice 10 i 11 kwiecień 1956*, 415–432.

Kwieciński, Piotr. 2001. *Disturbing strangeness.* Toruń: EDYTOR.

Łapicz, Czesław (ed.) 1994. *Polszczyzna dawna i współczesna. Materiały z ogólnopolskich konferencji językoznawczych.* Toruń: Wydawnictwo Naukowe Uniwersytetu Mikołaja Kopernika.

Makowski, Stanisław. 1969. *Świat sonetów krymskich Mickiewicza.* Warszawa: Czytelnik.

Mickiewicz, Adam. 1967. *Sonety krymskie* (with introduction and commentary by Janina Budzyńska). Wrocław: Ossolineum.

Mickiewicz, Adam. 1952. *Sonety krymskie* (with introduction and commentary by Roman Taborski). Wrocław: Ossolineum.

Mickiewicz, Adam. 1917. *Sonnets from the Crimea*, trans. by Edna Worthley Underwood. San Francisco: Paul Elder and Company Publisher. Project Gutenberg, http://www.gutenberg.org/files/27069/27069.txt, DOA February 10, 2011.

Mickiewicz, Adam. 1998. *The Sun of Liberty. Bicentenary Anthology 1798–1998.* Bilingual edition. Translated and edited by Michael J. Mikoś. Warszawa: Energia.

Newmark, Peter. 1988. *Approaches to Translation.* Cambridge: University Press.

Opacki, Ireneusz. 1972. *Poezja romantycznych przełomów.* Wrocław: Ossolineum.

Piechota, Marek (ed.) 1958. *Adam Mickiewicz. Materiały Śląskiej Sesji Mickiewiczowskiej Wyższej Szkoły Pedagogicznej Katowice 10 i 11 kwiecień 1956.* Katowice: Wydawnictwo Śląsk.

Raczyński, Edward. *Dziennik podróży do Turcji*, in Wacław Kubacki. 1977. *Z Mickiewiczem na Krymie*, 230.

Said, Edward. 1978. *Orientalism*, in Bill Ashcroft and Gareth Griffiths. 2009. *Post-colonial studies. The key concepts.*

Sawrymowicz, Eugeniusz. 1968. "Poetycka wizja Krymu w sonetach Mickiewicza", *Przegląd Humanistyczny* 5, 9–16.

Sękowski, Józef. 1824. *Collectanea z dziejów tureckich rzeczy do historii polskiej służących*, in Adam Mickiewicz. 1967. *Sonety krymskie* (with introduction and commentary by Janina Budzyńska). Wrocław: Ossolineum.

Słownik wyrazów obcych PWN. 2002. Warszawa: Wydawnictwo Naukowe PWN.

Słownik języka polskiego PWN. 2005. Warszawa: Wydawnictwo Naukowe PWN.

Szewczyk, Łucja M. 1994. "Nazewnictwo literackie w *Sonetach krymskich* Adama Mickiewicza", in Czesław Łapicz (ed.) *Polszczyzna dawna i współczesna. Materiały z ogólnopolskich konferencji językoznawczych*, 103–113.

Wyka, Kazimierz. 1893. *Wielka encyklopedia ilustrowana*, vol. IX. Warszawa, in Stanisław Makowski. 1969. *Świat sonetów krymskich Mickiewicza*.

Polish and English:
between translation and adaptation

Joanna Szakiel

Two audiences, two messages.
A case study of self-translation in *Fear / Strach* by Jan Tomasz Gross

Identity of the author / translator

The present paper aims to identify and categorize some of the most flagrant translation shifts between two language versions of a book by Jan Tomasz Gross (*Fear* in English, *Strach* in Polish), with particular emphasis on the socio-cultural context of the Polish and the American audiences. The case is especially interesting for three reasons: first, the author, despite Polish being his mother tongue, is a bilingual practicing self-translation; second, the two versions were practically written side by side, with the English book published earlier only due to a deadline imposed by the American publishing house; third, the books were preceded by *Sąsiedzi / Neighbors*, another dual publication on a similar topic, which gained extremely high profile in Poland, becoming a nexus of criticism and national debate. Thus, the case offers a chance to study two texts separated neither by time, nor the personality of the (re)writer, but very clearly by the target cultural context: the expectations of the target audience (or perhaps the author's perception of these expectations, given the previous reception of his work), and the author's emotional attitude to these two contexts (given his own complex sense of identity).

Jan Tomasz Gross, born in Warsaw in 1947 into a Polish-Jewish family of politically active intellectuals, grew up in "a very cosmopolitan milieu" (Silberklang 2001: 12). In 1968, as a political émigré he moved with his parents to the United States, where we earned a Ph.D. in sociology from Yale University. His scientific interests include "modern Europe, focusing on comparative politics, totalitarian and authoritarian regimes, Soviet and East European politics, and the Holocaust" (www.princeton.edu.pl). Gross identifies himself as "a Pole, a Jew and an American" (Kolenda-Zaleska, www.gala.pl), a sequence which seems non-accidental, for the author also declares that "[he is] first of all a Pole" [personal communication][1]. Polish roots and upbringing are also what determines

---

1 All quotations from my interview with Gross and from sources in Polish are my own translations. Czyżewski's paper is quoted on the basis of its English version from 2009.

his professional interests, since his "children speak Polish, [he] feels Polish and [he] never stopped to be concerned about Poland" (Hreczuk, www.polityka.pl). In an interview for the Polish Press Agency Gross confessed: "I wrote *Fear* as a Pole [...] The events described in *Fear* constitute an insult to my Polish identity" (Szwedowicz, www.naukawpolsce.pap.pl).

The identity and self-perception of the author is relevant, since just as Gross's publications received considerable attention from historians, the ensuing debates attracted the interest of numerous sociologists (Ciołkiewicz 2003, Czyżewski 2008) and anthropologists (Tokarska-Bakir 2003), the studies mainly pertaining to public and political discourse of the debate the books sparked and its potential ramifications for the phenomenon of so-called historical politics. Czyżewski observes that the debate over *Fear* was replete with "meta-discursive" aspects. Significantly, he considers the focus on the author's religious identity to be the most discernible of these tendencies. According to Czyżewski (2009: 147–148), Gross's self-identification as an author differs from the characteristics ascribed to him by many Polish recipients, which is to a large extent determined by the fact that *Fear* in the English language preceded its Polish version. The reckoning with the past it represents came to be interpreted through the prism of his Jewishness, in this context readily associated with what Norman Finkelstein would refer to as the 'Holocaust industry'. Ascribing particular importance to the author's biography not only shifted the focus from the actual content of the book, but evoked a set of negative connotations. In particular, "[t]he category of a 'Jew' (an 'American Jew') implied the issues of an easy academic and/or financial career, which allegedly was to be paved by means of a simplified and accusatory interpretation of the Holocaust" (148). Czyżewski (200: 149) indentifies this process as "ethnization" and "identity enforcement" predicated on an essential binary opposition between 'us' (Poles) and 'them' (Jews), therefore excluding Gross from the collectiveness of Polish society. The exclusion was necessary for many Poles, given the two-fold paradigm of treating Polish postwar history either through the prism of martyrology and romantic heroism, or as a blot on the national escutcheon.

Reception of *Sąsiedzi / Neighbors*

The two target audiences of Gross's books differ considerably not only in terms of their background knowledge and experience concerning the events described (which are set mostly in the context of wartime and post-war Poland) but, first and foremost, the emotional attitude towards them. Whereas in the United States the publications generally met with both critical and public acclaim, in Poland they proved extremely polarizing.

Neighbors (Polish: *Sąsiedzi*) was published in 2000 in Poland and, as a self-translation, a year later in the United States. It analyses the massacre of the Jewish community residing in the Polish town of Jedwabne. Gross meticulously describes systematic humiliation, torturing and harassment, which reached their apogee on 10 July 1941 when 1,600 Jews were herded into a local barn and subsequently burnt alive. The main controversy surrounding the book stems from the fact that, although the events presented take place at the peak of the Nazi regime, it is Polish civilians who are indicated as the sole perpetrators. The book sparked an unprecedented national debate, involving representatives of all cultural and political affiliations, media, as well as society at large, which has been referred to as "a watershed for Polish society" (Weinbaum 2002: 3) or "the most important debate of the free Poland" (Okoński 2011: 3). It heightened the tension between conservative and liberal visions of Polish history, in particular Polish-Jewish relations, and symbolically divided the public space into, to adopt Joanna Michlic's (2012) phrasing, the self-critical and the self-defensive. In a political dimension, the discussion reached its climax upon the decision by President Aleksander Kwaśniewski to take an official stance on the issue, when during the formal international celebrations of the sixtieth anniversary of the Jedwabne massacre, the head of the state apologized to the ambassador of Israel and paid homage to the victims (www.polish-jewish-heritage.org).

Among professional historians, the book was criticized, among other things, for the incorrect usage of archives, authoritative formulation of statements, affirmative approach towards sources, manipulation of the data and false accusations. A specimen of polemical and accusatory texts was published in a collection of essays by leading Polish historians, *Jedwabne. Spór historyków wokół książki Jana T. Grossa "Sąsiedzi"*. As Błażej Brzostek (2001: 1) observes, the main controversy surrounding *Neighbors* stems from the fact that it shifts the focus in the discussion of Holocaust from Polish-German to Polish-Jewish relations, therefore contesting the traditional self-perception of Poles as a heroic martyr-nation. Consequently, the book forces the reassessment of a time-honored image of Poland as a tolerant and hospitable country holding the highest number of Righteous Among the Nations and, instead, offers a more intricate view of Polish history. It instigated the revision of the perception of national history and the discussion of Holocaust that was no longer confined to intellectual discourse. Over a decade later, the echoes of the debate still resonate on many levels, and characterizing the public consternation over *Neighbors* as a landmark in modern Polish history does not seem to be an overstatement.

By contrast, the general public's reception of *Neighbors* in the USA was favorable, although it elicited professional reservations among certain historians.

Nevertheless, the issues of Gross's methodology and style, which constituted the dominant theme of critique in Poland, did not seem to generate a substantial amount of criticism from American commentators. In his review for *The New York Times*, Steven Erlanger called the book "an important contribution to the literature of human bestiality unleashed by war", at the same time, however, acknowledging its potential professional shortcomings. Naturally, the dispute about the book was also incomparably less confrontational than in Poland. In fact, the main source of criticism were representatives of Polish émigré intelligentsia who acted to prevent the alleged campaign against their motherland, with some members of the Polish diaspora demanding that the publisher withdraw from issuing and publicizing the book in the United States.

Reception of *Strach* / *Fear*

Fear, the book which will be the main subject of this paper, was published in the United States in 2006 under the full title *Fear: Anti-Semitism in Poland after Auschwitz: An Essay in Historical Interpretation* and in Poland as *Strach: antysemityzm w Polsce tuż po wojnie. historia moralnej zapaści*. In contrast to *Neighbors*, whose spatio-temporal framework was restricted to Jedwabne under the occupation, *Fear* explores the theme of anti-Semitism throughout Poland in the war and postwar period (with a particular emphasis on the latter). Its main and, at the same time, the most controversial argument is that the Polish prejudice against Jews was a nationwide phenomenon. As a background to the study of the 1946 Kielce pogrom, Gross describes such issues as psychological and physical humiliation, social exclusion, harassment and persecutions of Jews.

In Poland, its publication triggered a debate not only in historical, but also social and political circles. The book was even subjected to legal scrutiny and intervention of the church. Cardinal Dziwisz officially addressed the president of the publishing house which released the book. In his open letter to Henryk Woźniakowski, the Archbishop of Krakow points to the publisher's long religious traditions and suggests that, for ethical reasons, it should "take a closer look at the author's intentions" as *Fear* falsifies history and "awakens anti-Polish and anti-Semitic demons" (Dziwisz, www.kosciol.pl).

The debate over *Fear* served as a leading theme for a number of scientific meetings and conferences throughout the country. Predictably, it also generated considerable attention in the media. As in the case of *Neighbors*, the sharpest contrast of reactions to *Fear* can be observed between the dailies *Rzeczpospolita* and *Gazeta Wyborcza*. In *Rzeczpospolita*, historian Marek Jan Chodakiewicz takes issue with Gross's "collectivistic generalizations", erroneous research methods and postmodern approach to history. In the same newspaper, Ireneusz Krzemiński, a renowned sociologist exploring the Holocaust, states that *Fear* is neither strictly historical nor sociological and in fact classifies it as a "morality play" featuring a stereotyped and excessively emotional language, which, according to Krzemiński, may hinder Polish-Jewish dialogue.

A completely contradictory approach can be observed in the pages of *Gazeta Wyborcza*. Referring to the arguments on alleged historical deficiencies, for example, one of its leading journalists, Jarosław Kurski (2008: 16) stated that its loose narration and generalizations do not prevent *Fear* from offering credible historical references and a chance to change Polish collective memory of the Holocaust. Marek Beylin (2008: 2), from the same daily, states that although the book is not devoid of methodological flaws, "they are secondary compared to the challenge imposed by Gross on our reckoning with the past. (…) if it wasn't for *Fear*'s strained arguments and confrontational language, today's wide discussion about Polish anti-Semitism would not be possible. Just as one of the most important debates of Polish post-war period would not be possible without the pungency and over-generalizations of *Neighbors*".

In the United States, the book attracted considerable attention and received favorable reviews in the country's leading newspapers. American reviewers seem to differ considerably from Polish commentators in their treatment of Gross's methodology and his credibility as a historian. Such issues as criteria for the selection of sources, generalizations and simplifications, which attracted a great deal of negative publicity in Poland, are either presumed to be accurate, and therefore not requiring further (journalistic) investigation, or dealt with rather superficially. The press reviews which touch upon this problem seem to agree that *Fear* is a well-documented and scholarly study. David Margolick from *The New York Times*, for example, emphasizes the documentary importance of the book and mentions only minor reservations concerning the stylistic level:

> Ultimately, what's far more important than the "why" of this story is the "that": that a civilized nation could have descended so low, and that such behavior must be documented, remembered, discussed. This Gross does, intelligently and exhaustively. That he digresses from time to time, that his chronology can be confusing, that he repeats himself and occasionally lets his indignation get the better of him, doesn't really matter. (Margolick, www.nytimes.pl)

A recurrent feature is stressing the book's landmark role in redefining Polish historical self-image. Thane Rosenbaum, who reviewed the book for *Los Angeles Times*, predicts that *Fear* might play a greater role in the author's mother country than *Neighbors*, which described only a local phenomenon, for it "takes on an entire nation, forever depriving Poland of any false claims to the smug, easy virtue of an innocent bystander to Nazi atrocities." Rosenbaum's article also omits the question of Gross's historical methods. Instead, he adopts an emotional rhetoric on the book's paramount role in reshaping Polish national consciousness. In his view, the moral significance of *Fear* assumes an almost sublime quality ("The Holocaust is ultimately a ghost story, and Poles have many reasons to be haunted"); he seems to support the conviction that *Fear* encourages "national catharsis" and closes his review with the observation that "[i]t's never too late to mourn. The soul of the country depends on it" (www.articles.latimes.com).

Arguably, the most controversial commentary on *Fear* was delivered by Elie Wiesel, a Nobel Prize winner and Auschwitz survivor, globally recognized as one of the most influential Jewish thinkers in history (Cohn-Sherbok 1997: 127). In his review for *The Washington Post*, "The killing after the killing", Wiesel describes *Fear* as an important contribution to the study of the Holocaust, stressing the book's tremendous emotional impact. In highly emotional language, the review refers to the heated contemporary debate over the presence of non-Jewish religious symbols in Auschwitz Birkenau, in which Wiesel participated. The contentious review hinting at contemporary Polish anti-Semitism triggered reaction from Poland's ambassador to the United States, who replied to Wiesel's review with an open letter to *The Washington Post* editor. The favorable reception of *Fear* by mainstream American press also prompted an intervention of The Piast Institute, a prestigious think tank and research center for Polish and Polish American affairs. As a part of its anti-defamation program, the Institute launched an online symposium, where they addressed the book and the press coverage it generated in the United States, attempting to identify and rectify historical errors as well as undertake a polemic with alleged anti-Polish sentiments.

Fear: the two language versions compared

Since, as briefly accounted above, the reception of *Neighbors* in a way set the scene for the later reactions to *Fear* (and further publications by Gross), it may be assumed the author could envision some of the responses while producing the two versions of the book and perhaps preemptively take them into account. The paper will now examine the two versions, which, indeed, differ on several levels; in fact, the author makes an explicit statement that he does not feel obliged to follow the professional translator's code of conduct. Consequently, rather than "writing the same thing twice" (Gallant in Grutman 2013: 65), in the Polish version of the book, which he might expect to be subject to more scrupulous reading and more impassioned attacks, Gross places greater emphasis on historical and methodological validity, engaging in polemics with the newly produced data, incorporating commentaries and original quotes from his sources. At the same time, the books also differ in terms of the author's tenor and relationship with the audience. In the Polish text, his attitude tends to be more emphatic and personal but at the same time more judgmental; although the bilingual (self) translator is an intermediary between cultures, it is only in one language that he identifies himself with the audience.

One of the most frequently raised arguments against *Strach* (see chapter two) referred to the fact that its English edition preceded the Polish one. The author explains this choice with the level of knowledge of two target audiences. In *Neighbors*, Gross described events that had been largely unknown in Poland and consequently, he considered it reasonable that the Polish audience should be acquainted with the book first. By contrast, *Fear* touches upon a subject that Gross believed to be extensively investigated by professional historians and at the moment of publication already widely available to the Polish society at large [personal communication]. Gross explicitly addresses these objections in the following manner: "Przypomnę go [*Dziennik z lat okupacji Zamojszczyzny*] tutaj jeszcze raz, również i po to, aby uzmysłowić tym, którzy wyrazili niesmak, że *Strach* ukazał się najpierw po angielsku w Ameryce, że pisałem już o tych sprawach w Polsce po polsku pod koniec ubiegłego stulecia" (29), defending himself against the accusation that he is washing Poland's dirty linen abroad. The same argument seems to be applicable to the omission of the fragment concerning the Warsaw Uprising in the Polish version (in the English version presented in the chapter "The rhetoric of estrangement").

Nevertheless, Gross wrote certain fragments of *Fear* and *Strach* simultaneously, with precedence given to the English version only due to the deadline imposed by the publishing house. He also admits that he does not follow any definite pattern of producing two versions in different languages in any of his publications. Although Gross still regards writing in English more challenging than in his mother tongue, at the same time he stipulates that this hindrance is essentially of a linguistic nature. Therefore, his publications in the United States undergo stricter editorial review. In particular, Gross takes advice from experts as to the formal and stylistic idiosyncrasies of the English language ("to see if it reads well") [personal communication].

Textual layout and content rearrangement

From the point of view of the present thesis, the earliest harbinger of potential translation shifts becomes apparent already when comparing the books' titles: *Strach. Antysemityzm w Polsce tuż po wojnie. Historia moralnej zapaści* and *Fear.*

Anti-Semitism in Poland after Auschwitz. An essay in historical interpretation. It goes without saying that the Polish version seems to suggest a more severe approach ("a story of moral collapse") than an "essay in historical *interpretation*" [emphasis mine].

The books open with two quotes. The first one remains the same in both versions, the other differs significantly. The Polish opening, a short quotation from Hannah Arendt's *Personal responsibility under dictatorship,* is set in a rather contemplative mood, offering abstract philosophical insight on suffering and violence, whereas its English equivalent depicts a factual, brutal scene, from *We wish to inform you that tomorrow we will be killed with our families* by Philip Gourevitch:

> On April 30, 1997… Rwandan television showed footage of a man who confessed to having been among a party of genocidaires who had killed seventeen schoolgirls and a sixty-two-year-old Belgian nun at a boarding school in Gisenyi two night earlier. It was a second such attack on a school on a month; the first time, sixteen students were killed and twenty injured in Kibuye.
>
> The prisoner on television explained that the massacre was part of a Hutu Power "liberation" campaign… During [this] attack on the school in Gisenyi, teenage girls who had been roused from their sleep were ordered to separate themselves – Hutus from Tutsis. But the students had refused. At both schools, the girls said they were simply Rwandans, so they were beaten and shot indiscriminately.

This change may be motivated by Gross's intention to present the American audience with a more global perspective on the Holocaust by implying that the events described in *Fear* were not specific to the Polish culture but might have happened anywhere else, as "people all over the world undergo the same emotions and temptations" [personal communication]. Further examples of this strategy will be discussed below. The Polish edition also contains a dedication (as it was the case with *Neighbors*) and a note from the publisher with a very thought-provoking article written by the head of Znak publishing house, Henryk Woźniakowski.

The primary distinctive feature between the two versions, however, pertains to the complete change of content in the first chapters. The section called "Poland abandoned" (3) is replaced by a section under the very telling title "Ile milionów chrześcijan widziało z bliska mękę trzech milionów żydowskich współobywateli?" (19): an accusatory question asking how many Christians witnessed the suffering of their Jewish compatriots. On account of his belief that the Polish audience is already acquainted with the subject, Gross decided not to delve into the theme of the functioning of the Polish society under occupation, but instead to focus specifically on the situation of the Jews. However, he later admitted regretting that decision (Kolenda-Zaleska, 2013).

"Poland abandoned" provides necessary framework against which the main theme of the book is later to be mapped. Gross begins with the Ribbentrop-Molotov Pact (3) and guides the reader throughout the consecutive stages of the war, elaborating on such landmark events in Polish history as the conference in Yalta (14), the Warsaw Uprising (12) or the takeover by the Communist Party (22) as well as such specific terms as Armia Krajowa (5), Delegatura (5), the "Lublin Poles" (12), or "Three Times Yes" propaganda (23). By contrast, the Polish counterpart of the section principally concentrates on the suffering of Polish Jews, with personal testimonies (24–27) of several Holocaust survivors or observers (Maria Hochberg-Mariańska, Mojżesz Apelbaum, Szmukler Pikus, Samuel Rosenthhal), and particular focus on *Dziennik z lat okupacji Zamojszczyzny*, a well-known diary of Zygmunt Klukowski on the murdering of Jewish inhabitants of Szczebrzeszyn. The part also abounds in references to distinguished figures, including Mark Edelman (19), Milena Jasenska (19), Jan Karski (23) and Gustaw Herling Grudziński (46), and to memoirs by Poles who helped to save Jews (such as Antosia Wyrzykowska and Karolcia Sapetowa).

Naturally, therefore, the first chapters leave the two audiences with entirely different impressions. The introductory section of the English edition is written in an informative, dispassionate manner. The Polish version, by contrast, seems to represent an incomparably more emotional and judgmental account, as it plunges directly into the dramatic matter. To exemplify, the first chapter of *Strach* ends with the following conclusion:

> Bo Zagłada Żydów europejskich była całkowitą klęską zasad cywilizacyjnych, na których współcześnie oparte jest życie zbiorowe. Jedna z ponurych i powszechnie powtarzanych mądrości okupacji głosiła, że „po Żydach przyjdzie i na nas kolej". Nikogo chyba w Polsce nie trzeba przekonywać, że gdyby Hitler wygrał wojnę, do dzisiaj nie zostałoby śladu z polskiego społeczeństwa. I dlatego najważniejszym wyzwaniem wynikającym z doświadczenia drugiej wojny światowej, i to zarówno dla historii, jak i przyszłości Polski, jest zrozumienie, jacy ludzie, jakie tkanki społeczno-narodowego organizmu i za sprawą jakich mechanizmów okazały się podatne na zarażenie bakcylem nazizmu, którego integralną częścią składową była gotowość do pozbawienia życia drugiego człowieka tylko dlatego, że naziści pozwolili zabijać Żydów. (46)

Although subsequent (sub)chapters do not display such a degree of contrast, they also differ significantly, as suggested by their titles. The Polish ones commonly feature chilling quotations from witnesses and perpetrators of violence, testifying to the lack of empathy and moral scruples, while the English ones are merely informative labels corresponding to the content of the chapters. For instance, "Assault on the Building at Planty 7" labels the same chapter as "The child's mother was already dead anyway, so it would cry". Even the most unemotional of the

Polish titles seems more personal than its English counterpart (compare "Anti-Semitism among children" and "Anti-Semitism in schools").

Table 1: Chapter titles

Polish	English
„Moszek, to Ty żyjesz?" (47)	The unwelcoming of Jewish survivors (31)
Antysemityzm wśród dzieci (116)	Anti-Semitism in schools (66)
„Doszedłem do szofera i powiedziałem mu, że mamy Żydów i chcemy ich wywieźć, aby ich zabić" (129)	The Kielce pogrom: events (81)
„Matka i tak nie żyła już, więc dziecko by płakało" (160)	Assault on the Building at Planty 7 (85)
Mordowanie Żydów z braku innych zajęć (164)	Passionless killings (103)
„Nastroje w masach są na ogół dość negatywne"	The Kielce pogrom: reactions (118)
„Co ty mi będziesz opowiadała, psiakrew, wszyscy Żydzi są komunistami" (245)	Żydokomuna (192)

There is also no parallelism between analogous sections of *Strach* and *Fear*. The subchapter "Mord rytualny" (132), for example, does not appear in the English version as a self-contained section; parts of its content are instead spread throughout the book. An analogous phenomenon is present in the case of the chapter "The response of bishop Kubina", whose content in the Polish version is present in separate chapters. Besides the titles, Gross also does not preserve exact equivalence with respect to the order of individual subchapters. Still, what seems to be the most flagrant manifestation of "self-translator's authority" are the numerous elaborations, descriptions, and comments that appear alternately in only one of the two versions.

When the above is taken into consideration, it transpires that a comprehensive analysis of *Fear* shall include not only comparison between textually analogous fragments, but also identification of a given message even if it is conveyed in an inconsistent position in the other text. For instance, whereas the most important historical data are provided already in the opening sections of the text designated for the American audience, in the Polish edition the content is either truncated or interwoven into subsequent chapters. To exemplify, in the English version, Gross highlights that the widely quoted assessment of demographic losses during the Second World War is most likely an exaggeration for, in the light of contemporary research, the number oscillates around 5 million. In the Polish version this piece of information is provided on page 226. These rearrangements are, of course, not without an effect on the overall reception of the book's message.

The lack of close correspondence in terms of textual arrangement is especially visible in one of the most controversial theses put forward in the book, namely that the Catholic Church could have restricted the scale of killings of the Jews by Polish Catholics. However, in large part, the present study appears to contradict the arguments deployed by numerous Polish commentators stating that the Polish version is devoid of the most accusatory fragments concerning the Polish Church. Detailed comparative analysis of *Strach* and *Fear* proves that the said strings of text are, in fact, not excluded but replaced. This may be illustrated by the discrepancies between the location of portions of narrative concerning the disregard of the Church for the persecution of Jews. Significantly, in the English version the message (261) is divided into two parts (one of which is presented in the footnote) and featured in different chapters. In the Polish text (313–313), by contrast, it is placed in "Epilog", which brings closure to the work, and, therefore, may imply an intention to place stronger emphasis on this particular message.

Relationship with the audience

The references to the English version of the book, personal remarks, as well as the explicit address to the reader all contribute to the impression that, compared to *Fear*, the Polish edition is not only more direct, nuanced and involved, but also imbued with a greater emotional charge. This observation seems to be well illustrated by the following examples: "Co ty mi będziesz opowiadała, psiakrew, wszyscy Żydzi są komunistami!" about the concept of *żydokomuna* begins with a subchapter exclusive to the Polish version, in which Gross asserts: "W ten sposób, mam nadzieję, Czytelnicy sami będą mogli ocenić, czy mit 'żydowskiego komunizmu' ma jakiś związek z rzeczywistym postępowaniem Żydów", hoping the readers verify the stereotypical notion about Jews supporting and shaping the communist system. However, he further admits to doubts about his power to uproot the simplistic stereotype, and the willingness of some of his critics to change their minds:

> Ale wyznam od razu, że nie wiem, jak skutecznie prowadzić polemikę ze stereotypem, w dodatku obarczonym negatywną oceną – czyli zakorzenionym w świadomości społecznej uprzedzeniem (…) adresuję poniższą argumentację do Czytelnika, który gotów jest uznać, że żyjemy w czasach trudnych i skomplikowanych. (248)

In particular, this sense of intimacy in the Polish version is achieved through such linguistic features as the use of first person narrative. The author positions himself among those who need to frankly discuss the atrocities committed in their community, and to properly bury the dead:

> Aby się przed tym światem uchronić, musimy umieć ze sobą rozmawiać, zadawać pytania i wysłuchiwać udzielanych odpowiedzi. Stad nakaz zebrania wiedzy o masowej zbrodni, którą popełniono wśród nas. Po to żebyśmy tych tragicznie zmarłych mogli wreszcie przyzwoicie pochować. Nie tylko dlatego że tak się godzi, ale i dla własnego spokoju, żeby ich duchy przestały dręczyć nas i dzieci nasze głosami antysemitów i wyrzutów sumienia. (309)

Language and argumentation

Not only is the language of *Strach* more pungent, but it also seems to be more severe and judgmental. This occurrence seems best exemplified by the contrast between the more pejorative term "mord" and the more clinical "killing" in the English version, for example, in chapters "Mordowanie Żydów z braku innych zajęć" (164) and "Passionless killings" (103). Furthermore, the attitude of the author tends to be more ironic and, at times, also sarcastic in the text for the Polish audience.

Moreover, the argumentation of *Strach* is more complex and contains more explicit references to historical sources or historians and their works. The most representative example of this tendency seems to involve an open polemic with historian Andrzej Fabjański concerning the exact number of victims in the Kielce Pogrom. (161) For the illustration of the above statements on language and argumentation see the following examples:

Table 2: Extended argumentation in the Polish version

Polish	English
Instruktorzy KC bardzo podobnie przedstawiali dwa tygodnie później nastroje i tło wypadków. "W Kielcach w domu żydowskim mieszkało około 180 Żydów, którzy nie pracowali, wśród nich było tylko dwóch PPR-owców, w Ostrowcu kilkuset Żydów również nie pracuje. W większości uzdrowisk państwowych siedzą przeważnie bogaci Żydzi i reakcja polska" [reference]. *Innymi słowy, według oceny pracowników KC, Żydom się świetnie powodzi, chociaż nic nie robią, a przy tym ich obecność jest w ogóle denerwująca dla ludności miejscowej.* [my emphasis]	The July 19 report by the entire visiting delegation of Central Comittee instructors takes the matter further: "180 Jews were living in the Jewish building [Planty 7] in Kielce and they did not work; there were only two members of the PPR among them. In Ostrowiec several hundred Jews are also not working. In the majority of state-run spas one finds mostly rich Jews and Polish reactionaries". (124)
Sam zaś Berman opowiadał podczas wywiadu z Torańską, jak Stalin zwracał się czasami do niego i do Minca, przedrzeźniając żydowski akcent. "Według niego, nadawałem się na kosmopolitę" – powie Torańskiej, a jeszcze wcześniej, ze łzami w oczach, Stefanowi Staszewskiemu: "ja sam chodziłem ze stryczkiem na szyi, wiedziałem, że prędzej czy później pójdę na szafot". [reference] I choć te wyznania sfanatyzowanego żydowskiego inteligenta czytamy dziś z niesmakiem raczej niż ze współczuciem – bo jako nadzorujący bezpiekę członek Politbiura Berman był odpowiedzialny za zaciskanie "stryczka na szyi" tysiącom niewinnych ofiar, a samemu sobie założył stryczek wyłącznie na własne życzenie* – to z punktu widzenia oceny użyteczności pojęcia żydokomuny takie oświadczenie z wierzchołka piramidy władzy potwierdza wiedzę, którą uzyskaliśmy już z innych źródeł, że mianowicie pochodzenie żydowskie nikomu nie pomagało w karierze partyjnej. [*] Staszewski dodaje następujący komentarz podczas wywiadu z Torańską: "Nie jestem predysponowany do roli spowiednika, który ma udzielać rozgrzeszenia, bardzo źle się czułem w tej roli, więc powiedziałem: tak, wierzę, że wszyscy chodzili ze stryczkiem na szyi, tym bardziej że historia potwierdziła, iż byliśmy w przededniu nowej wielkiej czystki na skalę 1937 r., a może i większą. Ale nawet jeśli się chodzi ze stryczkiem na szyi, to nie jest dostateczny powód, żeby skazywać na śmierć niewinnych ludzi, nikogo nie może usprawiedliwiać fakt, że sam był zagrożony. I to był koniec naszej rozmowy z Bermanem" [reference]. (273)	"I was a cosmopolite soon to be discarded," Jakub Berman told journalist Teresa Torańska. After Stalin's crimes were denounced by Khrushchev at the Twentieth Congress of the Communist Party of the Soviet Union, Berman explained tearfully to a younger comrade that during Stalinism he had lived "with a noose around his neck". (290) [end-note] His interlocutor, who was also Jewish, replied that they had all had a noose wrapped around their necks but added that this did not exculpate Berman for what he had done as the Politburo member supervising the security apparatus. [reference]

The additional content visible in the table above consists of the author's reactions to and assessment of the sources he cites, and serves to highlight the main points of his argument. Especially the last of the quoted examples illustrates the tendency: in Polish, the sources are not only quoted more extensively, while in the English version the mention of Stalin imitating Jewish accent disappears, the first speaker is not reported to be close to tears, and the second speaker is not cited at all; they are also accompanied by remarks about the content (the first speaker is "fanatical" and guilty of persecution against "innocent victims"; his statement is read with "disgust rather than sympathy"), and about its meaning in the context discussed (i.e. Jewish background being a handicap rather than a key to success in the party).

At the same time, however, in numerous instances, the discourse of *Strach* seems to be more formal and emphatic than that of *Fear*. This is, for example, how in subchapter "Polemika ze stereotypem" (as mentioned above, present only in the Polish version) Gross elaborates on the notion of stereotype:

> Ale z drugiej strony, w odróżnieniu od generalizacji empirycznej, nie można stereotypu sklasyfikować za pomocą kontrprzykładu, przez powołanie się na fakty, które z uogólniającym sądem, jaki reprezentuje, nie dają się pogodzić. Inna metoda weryfikacji twierdzeń indukcyjnych – przez stawianie otaczającej rzeczywistości dodatkowych pytań i rozważanie, czy zjawiska skorelowane, które powinny być prawdziwe, jeśli stwierdzenie wyjściowe jest prawdziwe, znajdują potwierdzenie w faktach ("Jeśli Żydzi rządzą Polską, to dlaczego z niej uciekają", na przykład) – też wymaga otwartości na dialog i gotowości uznania, że życie społeczne jest urozmaicone. (247–248)

Still, the most flagrant discrepancies concern the manner of narration, which, despite a more intense relationship with the audience, tends to be more scientific and analytical in the Polish version. This trend, visible in the tone of the excerpt above, is often closely interwoven with a tendency to provide glosses and references to Holocaust context in the English version. Compare:

Table 3: Deliberation and description

Polish	English
Zapoznajmy się w tym celu z obrazem żydowskiego losu, jaki przyswoiło sobie w czasie okupacji polskie społeczeństwo. Co na temat Zagłady Żydów było wiadomo i w jaki sposób źródła podziemne pisały na bieżąco o tym, co się działo z Żydami? Z jednej strony, odpowiedź na te pytania jest bardzo prosta: było wiadomo wszystko, i to mniej więcej od razu. (…) Ale wiedza na temat otaczającej rzeczywistości, chociaż opiera się, naturalnie, na wrażeniach osobistych i obserwacjach, kształtuje się dopiero poprzez weryfikację, dyskusję i analizę. Musimy więc również wziąć pod uwagę, w jaki sposób o zarządzeniach i praktykach okupanta uderzających w ludność żydowską dyskutowano w obiegu publicznym, to znaczy w prasie konspiracyjnej i sprawozdaniach podziemnych. (227)	[Hence] a unique context in which the timing and the process of gaining awareness about the Holocaust needs to be noted with respect to Poland. Polish society had contemporaneous knowledge of the Holocaust – it knew about the mass murders of the Jews as they were taking place. Thus, when we investigate what was said about the Holocaust in Poland, and by whom, we must learn how this knowledge was registered and expressed. Unlike in France, Holland, the United States, or even Hungary, in Poland (but also in Russia, the Ukraine, Lithuania, Latvia, and Estonia) there is no mystery as to when and what people knew about the extermination of the Jews: they knew right away, and they knew pretty much everything there was to know. (169)
Odnotujmy wreszcie, że w standardowym heroicznym opisie czasów wojny występuje także jako swoisty wentyl bezpieczeństwa – uwiarygodniający zgodność z rzeczywistością – zdemoralizowany warunkami okupacji „margines społeczny", czyli wątek „szmalcownictwa". Taka konstrukcja narracji, w której eksploatacyjny aspekt stosunków polsko-żydowskich potraktowany jest jako „sprawa marginalna", jeszcze bardziej utrudniała zrozumienie, że oportunistyczne wykorzystanie możliwości stworzonych przez okupanta i udział w prześladowaniu żydowskich sąsiadów były zjawiskiem obejmującym stykających się z Żydami zwykłych mieszkańców miasteczek i wsi na obszarze całego kraju. (239)	Behavior that amounted to murderous assaults against Jews but that took place in urban contexts could not be ignored; and these acts are labeled in the narrative about wartime by a term with an unambiguously powerful negative connotation: *szmalcownictwo*. A *szmalcownik* was an extortionist who blackmailed Jews hiding on the Aryan side, threatening to reveal their whereabouts to the Nazis unless he (or she) was paid off. The concept conveniently marginalized the phenomenon and circumscribed it. "There is scum in every society", a standard commentary on the phenomenon informs us, rendering the story banal and uninteresting. Killings of village and shtetl Jews by their neighbors, on the other hand, have never made it into the historical consciousness of the epoch at all. (189)

While the excerpts above deal with similar topics, the concepts are critically discussed in Polish in academic register, with reference to the available sources and the metalanguage of history and sociology, while the English version focuses on merely establishing and describing the facts. Moreover, in numerous instances, in the Polish version Gross is more specific than in the English one. For example, examining the contemporary narrative adopted by Polish scholars with regard to the Catholic Church, in the English text he uses the collective expression "Church historians writing in Poland" (151); in the Polish version, however, he recalls specific names of such scholars (Gryz, Wrona, Śledzianowski, Żaryn) and provides references to their works (203). Similarly, the reaction of Polish intelligentsia to the Kielce pogrom is significantly more nuanced in the Polish version, with contributions by particular notable figures enumerated and discussed (214); since the figures would be probably anonymous to the Anglophone reader, they are only mentioned collectively (313).

The same trend is visible in the renditions of fragments about the ignorant attitude of cardinal Wyszyński (Polish: 135, English: 148) or cardinal Sapieha (Polish: 206, English: 139). Again, the attitude of Sapieha is even intensified in the Polish version, "dislike for Jews" becoming "antysemicki[e] pogląd[y]" ("anti-Semitic views"). While in the Polish edition the chapter describing the reactions of the Catholic clergy to the Kielce pogrom contains direct quotations of the homilies (190), *Fear* builds only on their paraphrases (136). Similarly, the report by Kaczmarek is presented verbatim in Polish only, and then in a more abridged form in the Polish (193) and the English (142) version respectively.

Nevertheless, there are at least two instances where potentially controversial fragments are not incorporated into the Polish edition. The first fragment refers to the confidential document issued by the Holy See to Angelo Roncalli, the papal nuncio in France, which stipulated that Jewish children who had been entrusted to Catholic institutions can only be surrendered back to their parents if they had not been baptized. Gross comments on these procedures as follows: "In the matter of ritual murder accusations, we may identify a directly associated reverse practice which has never been widely discussed as a contested issue of Catholic-Jewish relations. I have in mind the 'ritual murder' of Jewish children by Catholic clergy, which took place, in a manner of speaking, every time a Jewish child was baptized without a specific request or authorization by his or her parents" (162). Another facet relevant to the framework of academic credibility pertains to the manner of presenting historical data. For instance, Gross extrapolates that the number of "beneficiaries" of the disappearance of Jews provided by Lizak may be higher, but he proposes the exact figure only in the English version. The former omission may be connected to the more international and universal perspective assumed by the Anglophone version (see below).

Moreover, in a non-scientific field, especially when touching upon the topic of moral responsibility for the suffering of Jews, the narrative of *Strach* seems to contain more esoteric and religious references, which seek to illuminate the powerful emotional and moral meaning of the discussed events. Jews returning to reclaim their property (298) are described to have been viewed as akin to "vampires", "returning from beyond the grave", a psychologically repressed "symbol of sin", demanding "examination of conscience" (a Catholic confessional term for a review of one's actions before penance). In the English version, the allusions are absent and the description is much reduced (256), although, interestingly, the proximity between the murderers and their victims is then elaborated by employing ethnologist and anthropologist perspectives. Gross introduces the concept of pseudospeciation developed by Jane Goodall, an eminent authority on the study of primates, to explain the phenomenon of victims being "relegated to nonhuman status" (253). The author devotes a considerable space to describe Goodall's work with chimpanzee communities in Africa to ultimately adapt her findings to the context of "cultural speciation".

Argumentation: the universal and the local

The primatologist perspective seems symptomatic since, as already signaled, in contrast to the Polish text, the English version tends to present the phenomenon described in the book in a more global context. Elaborating on the notion of "cultural or social speciation as a process of acquiring national consciousness", Gross adds the following quotation:

> The writer Brian Hall was told by a Muslim man from Bosnia: "Five years ago I never even thought about who was who. Croat? Serb? Muslim? Why would I care about something like that? I didn't even know what some of my friends were. What really frightens me – and even more than that, what *amazes* [emphasis in the original] me – is how quickly the tribal feelings have arisen". (255)

Moreover, in order to explain some of the most perplexing concepts, Gross adapts them to a specifically American context. When discussing the sociological complexity of the Kielce pogrom, for example, he makes the following comparison:

> Familiar categories are not easily applicable to this story. (...) One should rather turn to lynching as a useful concept for grappling with such a reality. As to the canard of Jews killing Christian children for blood, which so effectively mobilized people for action, it is perhaps analogous to the imaginary terror of "southern whites, [who] in their belief that black men were preoccupied with having intercourse with white women, were

largely battling a monster of their own creation: the long-standing sexual access to black women that white men had enjoyed." (163)

Naturally, the American version tends to be more descriptive and explanatory. It abounds in definitions of concepts such as *Odrodzenie* (Reneissance) (168), *Arrow Cross Party* (224), *sanacja* (198), *Hersh Smolar* (219) or *bezpieka* (228). Furthermore, in the English version numerous explanations are embedded with an additional commentary, such as "This is a very complex theme made up of multiple strands", which is then followed by an elaborate explanation of the process of productivization. Similarly, certain comments are equipped with directions for correct interpretation, e.g. "This should not be read as […]" caveat when explaining the intricacies of Communist propaganda (123, 124). The English edition also contains more explanations by comparison, such as, for example: "The functioning of the Communist secret police had nothing to do with Jews (or Poles) – it operated just as smoothly and followed a similar blueprint in Albania, East Germany, Cuba, China, and North Korea" (230), again giving the events a more universal, human perspective. As already indicated by the book's opening, these include references to more contemporary atrocities, such as the quotation from *Becoming Evil*:

> 'Everyone was called to hunt the enemy', said Theodore Nyilinkwaya, a survivor of the massacres in his home village of Kimbogo, in the southwestern province of Cyangugu. 'But let's say someone is reluctant. Say that guy comes with a stick. They tell him, "No, get a masu." So, OK, he does, and he runs along with the rest, but he doesn't kill. They say, "Hey, he might denounce us later. He must kill, Everyone must help to kill at least one person." So this person who is not a killer is made to do it. And the next day it's become a game for him. You don't need to keep pushing him.' (252)

Conclusion

As opposed to regular translation, self-translation offers the rewriter an incomparable degree of freedom. As Gross states in his introduction to the Polish version of *Fear*, as an author acting in the role of a translator, he did not feel obliged to preserve literal uniformity of both texts. Indeed, his position on the treatment of self-translation seems to coincide with the general theoretical premise which assumes that "where the author and the translator are one and the same person, the requirements of 'faithfulness to the original' no longer apply" and, consequently, that such status confers upon the author the "liberty to emend, to elaborate" (Grayson in Woods 2006: 15). Making use of this freedom, and of his dual identity, the author provides two distinct perspectives on the events he describes: a more universal one for the American readership, marked by a more popular tone of the work; and a more impassioned and personal tone for the Polish reader.

References

Beylin, Marek. "Żydzi, Polacy, Strach", http://wyborcza.pl/1,87771,4831168.html, DOA April 2, 2013.

Ciołkiewicz, Paweł. 2003 "Debata publiczna na temat mordu w Jedwabnem w kontekście przeobrażeń pamięci zbiorowej" in *Przegląd socjologiczny* 1/2003, 285–306.

Cordingley, Anthony (ed.) 2013. *Self-translation: Brokering originality in hybrid culture.* London: Bloomsbury Academic.

Czyżewski, Marek. 2009. "Polish Debate around *Fear* by Jan Tomasz Gross from the Perspective of the Intermediary Discourse Analysis", in Ruth Wodak and Gertraud Auer Borea d'Olmo (eds.) *Justice and Memory. Confronting Traumatic Pasts. An International Comparison,* Vienna: Passagen Verlag.

Erlanger, Steven. "Hitler's willing executioners", http://www.nytimes.com/books/01/04/08/-reviews/010408.08erlangt.html, DOA March 27, 2013.

Gross, Jan Tomasz. 2000. *Sąsiedzi: Historia zagłady żydowskiego miasteczka.* Sejny: Fundacja Pogranicze.

Gross, Jan Tomasz. 2001. *Neighbors: The Destruction of the Jewish Community in Jedwabne, Poland.* Princeton: Princeton University Press.

Gross, Jan Tomasz. 2006. *Fear: Anti-Semitism in Poland After Auschwitz.* New York: Random House.

Gross, Jan Tomasz. 2008. *Strach: Antysemityzm w Polsce tuż po wojnie. Historia moralnej zapaści.* Kraków: Znak.

Gross, Jan Tomasz and Irena Grudzińska-Gross. 2011. *Złote żniwa. Rzecz o tym, co się działo na obrzeżach zagłady Żydów.* Kraków: Znak.

Gross, Jan Tomasz and Irena Grudzińska-Gross. 2012. *Golden Harvest.* New York: Oxford University Press.

Gross, Jan Tomasz. 2003. *Wokół „Sąsiadów": polemiki i wyjaśnienia.* Sejny: Pogranicze.

Grutman, Rainier. 2013. "A sociological glance at self-translation and self-translators", in Anthony Cordingley (ed.) *Self-translation: Brokering originality in hybrid culture,* 63–81.

Kolenda-Zaleska, Katarzyna. "Jan Tomasz Gross: Nie burzę mitów", http://www. gala.pl/-gwiazdy/wywiady/zobacz/artykul/jan-tomasz-gross-nie-burze-mitow. html, DOA April 3, 2013.

Kurski, Jarosław. 2013. "Powiedzieli o Strachu", http://www.archiwum.wyborcza.pl/-Archiwum/1,0,5015669,20080119RPDGW,POWIEDZIELI_O_ STRACHU.html, DOA April 2, 201.

Michlic, Joanna. 2002. "Coming to terms with the Dark Past. The Polish debate about the Jedwabne massacre". Acta (21). Jerusalem: Hebrew University of Jerusalem.

Okoński, Michał. 2011. "Archeologia stodoły", http://tygodnik.onet.pl/kraj/archeologia-stodoly/5lx1b, DOA March 22, 2013.

Rosenbaum, Thane. "A lethal homecoming", http://articles.latimes.com/2006/ jun/25/-books/bk-rosenbaum25, DOA February 27, 2013.

Silberklang, David. "Interview with Jan Tomasz Gross", http://www.yadvashem. org/-about_HOLocaust/studies/vol30/gross.PDF, DOA March 22, 2013.

Szwedowicz, Agata. "Gross: pisałem Strach jako Polak". http://naukawpolsce. pap.pl/-aktualnosci/news,69889,gross-pisalem-strach-jako-polak.html, DOA April 17, 2013.

Tokarska-Bakir, Joanna. "Strach w Polsce", http://wyborcza.pl/1,111789,4830844. html, DOA April 3, 2013.

Wiesel, Elie. "Killing after the killing", http://www.washingtonpost.com/wp-dyn/ content/-article/2006/06/23/AR2006062301304.html, DOA April 5, 2013.

Weinbaum Laurence, "Penitence and Prejudice: The Roman Catholic Church and Jedwabne" in: Jewish Political Studies Review. Fall 2002. 14, 3–4.

Woods, Michelle. 2006. "Translating Milan Kundera". Topics in translation. London: Multilingual Matters.

Aleksandra Borowska

Localizing a new text-type. Anglophone Internet memes and their Polish versions

The concept of a meme

The purpose of the paper is to explore and describe the phenomenon of Anglophone Internet memes and their Polish versions. The topic does not appear to have received a lot of academic attention, hence the reliance on Internet sources discussing Anglophone Internet memes and their Polish versions, which the paper tries to present in the context of translation and localization. First, the phenomenon will be described. Conventions and mechanics related to Internet memes will be discussed; examples of meme life cycles will be presented and explained. Then, I will present the phenomenon of meme translation, including the factors determining the fitness of memes, treating them as "cultural genes". Possible translation issues which may stem from different layers of Internet memes, such as the text, the image, and the culture-specific items will also be discussed, as well as translation methods employed by Polish users.

The dawn of the 21st century and the widespread use of the Internet have created a reality in which content created by users appears simultaneously all over the world and terabytes of information are exchanged every second. Since geographical boundaries no longer matter as much as before, when memes spread, they are not limited by space, and gradually less so by time. In the second decade of the 21st century Internet memes are a very popular, although seemingly novel medium of communication, varying in their theme, register and form. Sources related to the idea of translating memes seem to be rather scarce, rendering it necessary to research whether they are really such a new concept, or perhaps a well established one, yet adapted to the reality of Web 2.0 and other contemporary technologies. Certainly they can be summarized to "rely heavily upon the postmodern themes of intertextuality, pastiche, subversion, reflexivity, and obscurity" (Gage http://cylegage.com).

The term *meme* itself is inspired by Richard Dawkins's description of concepts "leaping from brain to brain" (Dawkins 1989: 192) and subject to three processes: replication, mutation, and propagation, which cause their evolutionary changes. In a contemporary context, replication is facilitated by media which enable instantaneous sharing of information. Numerous users repeat and resend the same piece of news or gossip independently. Since every cultural artefact is altered at some point in the process of replication, memes are subject to mutation. For example, the basic structure of a narrative may remain the same, that is: a champion arises, battles an antagonist and receives a reward. Over time, however, both the heroes and the settings need updating. Certain sub-plots or character archetypes are preserved and prominent in a particular time-frame and change with the spirit of successive generations. This implies that there are qualities in every meme which determine its 'fitness' and 'survivability'.

As Dawkins puts it, "leaping from brain to brain" involves both replication, here understood as copying content from one mind to another, and mutation, as the replicated meme is individually processed, understood and repeated in a different context. There exist numerous groups of more or less independent users who may or may not interact with one another, as the meme branches out, in theory, indefinitely. A cultural artefact, such as a story, is told and heard by a certain number of individuals. Some may seek to replicate it as best they can, others might decide to add their own content and then propagate the mutated result, making it available to more users. Translation – or localization – of content is obviously one of the means by which a meme may spread and mutate, and any shifts occurring in the process of translation are likely to influence a meme's chances for survival. Translation, in this case, seems to be the closest to the process of propagation.

Internet memes

In the Internet context, an attempt to describe the viral phrases, pictures, and clips known as 'memes' has been made by "Know Your Meme", a user-generated database which will be further referred to as KYM, containing information on the origin of various memes, possible uses and appropriate contexts, examples of replications and approximate time-frames of popularity (http://knowyourmeme. com/).

The existence of such a website emphasises users' drive to catalogue Internet phenomena. The site proposes a division into confirmed memes and those still being researched. The origin, range, usage, imitations and derivatives of every meme are discussed on a dedicated subpage, allowing the meme's lifecycle to be tracked across various online communities. The idea of usage is particularly interesting as it implies that Internet memes are not only absurd images paired with amusing captions. Usage suggests that certain memes may have a semantic quality of their own and may be used as a reply to an utterance or a comment. The aforementioned quality adds a non-verbal semantic layer to the features of Internet memes, giving them a symbolic value, even when there is no caption present, which allows to differentiate between several subtypes. The proposed categories would be: reaction faces, demotivational posters, image macros (including, but not restricted to Advice Animals), snowclone templates, and derivatives of all the above types.

The lifecycle of memes can be illustrated on the example of a reaction face picture known as 'Me Gusta' or 'Me Gusta Face'. Literally 'I like it' from Spanish, the phrase used as a meme initially "conveyed an odd sense of pleasure in sexually perverse contexts, but the meaning has since broadened to describe a more general state of being disturbed and pleased at the same time www. knowyourmeme.com).

The meme originated in 2010, first on 4chan, then on reddit. Google Trends presents its gradual growth in popularity starting in April 2010 with two periods of intense growth, between January and April 2011 and from September 2011 to February 2012, when its popularity peaked. Despite a noticeable decline in popularity, 'Me Gusta' retains a steady number of search hits. Most likely, the reason behind it is the possible usage of the meme as a reaction in online conversations or a comment on submitted content, for example on social networking websites such as Facebook.

Figure 1: "Me gusta" face: standalone and incorporated into context

Templates and meme variation

Another Internet meme used as a case study for life cycles represents the category of picture and caption templates, also known as snowclone templates. The latter term originated in a series of blog posts on Language Log. The author, Geoffrey K. Pullum from the University of Edinburgh, discussed the need to name "a multi-use, customizable, instantly recognizable, time-worn, quoted or misquoted phrase or sentence that can be used in an entirely open array of different jokey variants by lazy journalists and writers" (Pullum 2003). One of the phrases exemplifying the term would be "X is the new Y". Pullum elaborated on the usage in the following excerpt:

> If Eskimos have N words for snow… (pick any number you like for the N), especially as the first sentence in a piece. It has become a journalistic cliché phrase with an attention-grabbing hook and totally free parameters for you to set as you wish – that is, the value for N and the main clause that you continue the sentence with (like …Santa Cruzans must have even more for surf or whatever). (Pullum 2003)

Pullum himself claimed that the term cliché was insufficient. In response, Glen Whitman from the California State University opted to call "these non-sexually reproduced journalistic textual templates" snowclones, which Pullum accepted (2004). Many Internet memes follow this definition so closely that their respective entries in the KYM database use a similar algebraic notation. A meme which originated in 2010 on the *Hyberbole and a Half* blog may be used as an example. (http://knowyourmeme.com/memes/x-all-the-y)

Figure 2: "X all the Y"

Memes may cross-reference other memes and meme templates to evolve new meanings. As an illustration of how the template itself may change the understanding of the message, a reddit user called OblviousTrollAccount posted a collage picture of different Advice Animal memes, each captioned with an almost identical sentence (2.03.2013, www.reddit.com), yet with different connotations. "Advice Animals", memes using an image template, be it a colour wheel background or a photo, usually of a person or an animal. The template displays independent semantic value and may alter the interpretation of the caption as shown below (names of the presented memes have been taken from their respective subpages on knowyourmeme.com)

Starting from top left, the "Good Guy Greg" interpretation suggests a comfortable situation which rids one of the need to change names in the documents after becoming married. The middle picture in the top row uses the "Overly Attached Girlfriend" template, which is usually connected to a feeling of unease, caused by rather possessive assumptions made by one's partner in a relationship. Next, "Redneck Randall", a culturally specific meme mocking stereotypes pertaining to the inhabitants of the southern parts of the United States, seems to allude to the idea of possible incestuous marriage.

The two pictures from the middle row are derivatives of their respective base memes, namely "Socially Awkward Penguin", with a blue background, and "Socially Awesome Penguin", with a red background. In their basic forms, they present behaviours that (in the former case) the creators deem to be displays of social ineptitude, or decisions that, although potentially risky, result in a most appealing turn of events (in the latter case). The derivatives present a mixture of a seemingly pleasing situation with a rather embarrassing conclusion and vice versa, depending on the interpretation.

Figure 3: Variations on "We already have the same last name"

"Scumbag Stacy", the rightmost picture in the middle row, semantically represents a woman whose actions may be perceived as intentionally destructive and evil. Interestingly enough, it is already a mutation of the "Scumbag Steve" meme, which features Stacy's male counterpart and predecessor. In this rendition, the sentence can be read as the woman taking pride in depriving her husband of the possibility to give her his last name. The memes in the bottom row, starting from the left, are "First World Problems" and "Sudden Clarity Clarence". The former mocks preoccupation with insignificant issues, such as the lack of wireless network access while waiting for a flight to a holiday destination. The latter meme uses the picture of a bewildered, wide-eyed young man in a moment of unexpected epiphany.

Translation of Internet memes

Internet memes (ranging from raw pictures, catchphrases, captioned pictures and their subtypes, to short animations and viral videos) usually aim to mock, subvert or ridicule a given theme, phenomenon, behaviour or person for the amusement of the users. Universal situations, features of character or stereotypes are very often a source of inspiration, contentwise. Memes pertaining to themes which transcend cultural borders are more than likely to be replicated and propagated by various communities. On the other hand, culturally or linguistically specific memes, relying on shared knowledge and a high level of intertextuality tend to be appreciated by smaller communities or within a linguistically hermetic group, where they are subject to further mutations, depending on how specific they eventually become.

Both types of Internet memes spread from their place and time of origin through numerous channels. One way or another, they are brought to communities where English is not the first, second or otherwise a widely known language, thus inciting the demand and need to be translated. The translation of Internet memes presents a variety of possible issues which may relate to the intended meanings, linguistic creativity, cultural references or a combination of these factors. Since a meme's success depends primarily on how recognizable it becomes for the users, such features as linguistic creativity, exemplified by puns, intentional misspellings, wordplay, or the use of non-standard language varieties, seems to be a significant factor in the popularity of a meme and its reception. In the face of such challenges, most of the content requires an individual approach, with methods ranging from literal word for word translation, through minor alterations of language, to creative adaptation or translation through the use of culture-specific equivalents, which approach localization or transcreation. The following sections will examine the ways in which memes as a text-type as well as particular derivative memes function in the Polish context.

Internet memes amongst speakers of Polish

Certain conventions need to be established in order to commence the explanation of how Internet memes function amongst speakers of Polish. In comparing their form and content in relation to those in the source language one may observe certain criteria of meme fitness, which would correspond to Gideon Toury's notion of acceptability.

Even without formal training in translation, users observe certain standards and may adhere to a set of conventions naturally, especially if certain elements, such as the layout, or the background, are reinforced and propagated. Awareness of the form seems particularly important when it comes to mutation, where users seek to create their own templates and attempt to make them similar to existing memes in order to increase fitness and facilitate the text-type identification of their submissions.

The creation and translation of Internet memes appears to be governed by naturally developed standards. Gideon Toury proposed the idea of translation norms in his work, *Descriptive Translation Studies and Beyond* (1995: 53–64). One of the aspects which Toury discusses is the question of adequacy versus acceptability and defines the difference as follows:

> [A]dherence to source norms determines a translation's adequacy as compared to the source text, subscription to norms originating in the target culture determines its acceptability. (56–57)

Anyone who is willing to undertake the translation effort does not only change the text's language but may also transform (i.e. the genre, format, template), appropriating it into a form which appears to be more acceptable in the target culture. The translator enables the speakers of the target language to have access to viral pictures or videos which would otherwise remain incomprehensible for them as the translated content becomes submitted to locally known websites or social media communities.

The process of adopting the text to target norms is organic. The translation of Internet memes as user created content does not require any form of official approval (unless it is submitted to a website which follows a set of content restrictions), nor are memes formally controlled or reviewed when translated. Of course, other users have the opportunity to evaluate a submission by means of comments or a voting system (as present, for example, on reddit). All in all, it is important to remember that Internet memes are a form of user-created content and their translation also appears to be done by users. While one can assume the translators to possess a certain degree of linguistic competence, they cannot be assumed to be professional translators, familiar with the range of available procedures, let alone translation theories. This is in keeping with Toury's vision of norms as emergent social phenomena, and the union of creators and audience makes acceptable translations (or localizations) of memes a particularly interesting case to research. There are certain similarities between the structure of Internet memes and, for example, posters or advertisements, as Internet memes can be considered short forms, usually consisting of a catchphrase, a single utterance or a group of words closely related to an image. The elementary difference, however, lies in the source of Internet memes. The common ground for creators of Internet memes is their access to the Internet, awareness of the existence of the discussed phenomenon and the initiative to caption an existing template or introduce a new template. It is the users (of various backgrounds) who are the creators of Internet memes, while posters or advertisements are usually created by marketing professionals or artists; in the case of memes, user-translators can be expected to be singularily attuned to the norms created by other users. The examples below illustrate such a change into more conventional target forms.

Polish versions of Anglophone memes

On 7th October 2013, a video titled "Telekinetic Coffee Shop Surprise" was uploaded on Youtube by a user under the name of CarrieNYC (www.youtube.com). The description of the video is as follows: "What if telekinesis was real? How would you react? Our hidden camera experiment captures the reactions of unsuspecting customers at a New York City coffee shop as they witness a telekinetic event". The last seconds of the video contain frames from the movie and the release date. The video quickly reached reddit and spread throughout blogs and social media. On 8th October 2013, user Dixx37 submitted the same video embedded in the frame of a demotivational poster to the Polish website www. demotywatory.pl. The added caption, as visible below, could be translated as "A prank in a cafe as a movie preview will attract more people to cinemas than most advertisements would". The user who submitted the Polish version of the viral video did not translate the text included in the original upload but added a new caption which explains the story and intention behind the video. It appears that the user chose to host the submission at demotywatory.pl (which according to a December 2012 survey by wirtualnemedia.pl was the most popular Polish website with humorous content, with 3.3 million users), and applied the associated format in order to increase the fitness of this meme.

Figure 4: "Telekinetic Coffee Shop Surprise"

The user who reuploaded the content as a demotivational poster did not seem to be concerned with the adequacy in a word for word translation of the description (or, for that matter, with correct spelling). Instead, the focus was shifted into making the video available to a possibly multi-million Polish speaking audience on a known website.

Another example of popular content which was remade into a demotivational poster could be a transformation of reddit.pl content into a demotywatory.pl submission. On 25ᵗʰ September 2013, user hamburgersandwiches posted a link to a digital photo album on imgur.com in a post titled "Fuck it. I'm getting married Saturday. Here are my crappy engagement photos" (reddit.com), which contained frames from various films with the faces of himself and his girlfriend edited onto the pictures. On 26ᵗʰ September 2013, user holdOn reuploaded the images into an album on demotywatory.pl titled: "You will never be this fucking awesome" ("Nigdy nie będziesz tak zajebisty" in Polish). The original uploader refers to the photos as "crappy" (of subpar quality), perhaps out of modesty or embarrassment; the intention behind the vocabulary choice appears unclear and may be ironic. By contrast, the tone of the caption in Polish seems to imply that efforts undertaken by prospective spouses to commemorate their engagement will never be as original, and thus the submission may intend to demotivate the readers. Once again, the acceptability of a form firmly established in the consciousness of Polish users takes precedence over the adequacy of the translation and appears to illustrate Toury's law of growing standardization, where "source-text textemes tend to be converted into target-language (or target-culture) repertoremes" (1995: 267–268).

Conventions in Polish Internet memes

Demotivational posters, discussed above, appear to be amongst the most popular meme forms on the Polish Internet but several other genre conventions seem to be well established and in use. News websites seem to have embraced the idea of Internet memes and present user-made comments in galleries, as exemplified by tvn24.pl and their article containing images made after Pope Francis was elected in early 2013 (tvn24.pl), making Internet memes a means of social and cultural communication. Apart from pre-existing templates, there exists a rather noticeable pool of memes which originated within the Polish language and culture. Often, an influx of new memes or replications of existing templates may be observed after events which receive significant media coverage (Olympics in London, Royal Baby). The section below will briefly discuss reaction faces and rage comics, image templates and snowclones.

Reaction faces and rage comics could be categorised as Internet memes which are the easiest to use and exploit in user-created content. Templates can be freely combined and captions can be added in order to produce a context-relevant meme. Sites such as komixxy.pl (voted fourth most popular humour-related website in Poland in 2011) allow users to quickly create several frames of a webcomic with the use of templates, often containing rage comics and similar simple memes. Effectively, the used memes have become established and identifiable by the Polish users of Internet who either access the website or view content produced there and shared through social media. The tab "Postacie" (Characters) serves as a database of meme templates on komixxy.pl. It contains the most popular images, appropriately labelled. Interestingly enough, certain templates, such as "Mother of God", used to "express astonishment or disbelief in response to a shocking image or a video" (knowyourmeme.com) are labelled in English, while the text in the picture appears in Polish, as in the image below. The version found on komixxy.pl appears to be a slightly modified version of the template shown by knowyourmeme.com; in the English version the caption is placed above the drawn face, the font is red, and the phrase is followed by an ellipsis mark.

Figure 5: "Mother of God"

Polish users appear to have embraced the idea of image macros, since numerous replications of internationally known templates as well as original ones can be found in use. The popularity of Internet memes naturally led to the founding of websites which allow users to quickly generate memes and share them online. One of such websites, fabrykamemow.pl, lists memes and the number of their variants, providing a short explanation concerning the semantics of the template and the most popular replications. As such, the site significantly facilitates meme production and provides textual knowledge on the genre.

One of the administrators, under the username "coldseed", states that in naming Polish versions of the memes, the administrators focus on conveying the associations rather than a faithful translation of the original name. For instance, "Stoner Stanley", a meme showing an incoherent marijuana smoker, in the Polish version features the Polish name Zbyszek, which preserves the alliteration and seemed to intuitively fit the "charming" character (private e-mail, August 29, 2013[2]).

Apart from translated memes, the site illustrates the popularity of target culture-related content. The examples below present four templates with at least 1,000 replications each. Starting from top left, they were named "Napuszony Jarosław", "Bogusław Linda", "Magdalena G." and "Suchy Karol".

---

2   „Jeśli chodzi o tytuły szablonów, czyli memowych postaci to bardziej nad dosłowne tłumaczenie postawiliśmy oddanie sensu danej serii obrazków. Sztandarowym przykładem jest 'Stoner Smiley', czyli postać upalonego zielskiem młodzieńca, któremu język się plącze, a jego nieskładne wypowiedzi świadczą o szwankującej pamięci krótkotrwałej. Szablon ten nazwaliśmy 'Zjaranym Zbyszkiem' – imię Zbyszek jest po prostu urocze i idealnie nam pasowało do Stanley'a. Często jest tak, że nie zwracamy nawet uwagi na oryginalne nazwy szablonów i na podstawie funkcji jaką spełnia przedstawiona w memie postać, staramy się wybrać najbardziej trafną nazwę. Robimy to bez rad tłumacza, ma się rozumieć. Zdajemy się na własną intuicję.:)".

Figure 6: "Napuszony Jarosław" (top left); "Bogusław Linda" (top right); "Suchy Karol" (bottom left); "Magdalena G." (bottom right)

The Internet memes in the top row could be examples of snowclone templates, with the set phrases being "Wina Tuska" and "Ja Wam Ku**a Dam" respectively. The first shows a politician who attributes all disasters, maladies and unpleasant events to his political opponent, against a background reminiscent of that used for advice animals. The second example uses the image of a Polish actor, Bogusław Linda, known for playing violent, hardened characters. The snowclone phrase, "Ja Wam Ku**a Dam", containing an expletive, can be used to expresses an extremely hostile attitude to events or people. The third example, "Suchy Karol", appears to have become the Polish substitute for image macros such as "Lame Pun Coon" or "Bad Joke Eel" as a means of consciously presenting unfunny jokes, based on polysemy or homophony. The meme refers to Karol Strasburger, the host of a popular Polish quiz programme, who is known for opening the show with such puns, and *suchy* refers to *suchar*, a term for a stale, poor joke. Finally, the bottom right template, "Magdalena G.", ridicules the critical remarks of a gourmet and restaurant owner, Magdalena Gessler, who hosts a television programme dedicated to revitalising unsuccessful restaurants.

All of the memes presented above refer to people who are considered public figures, either because of their position or the presence in the media. Fabrykamemow.pl also contains templates relating to various stereotypes, such as bait-and-switch memes or references to various national vice, which appear to be successfully adopted and established in Polish replications. For example "Typical Polish Tourist" (Typowy Polski Turysta) depicts an ignorant penny-pinching man who wears socks with sandals. This may be a localized version of such American culture-specific templates as "Redneck Randall"; while such American memes are not replicated, they seem to have mutated into a form which mocks very similar behaviours, based on the observations of local culture.

Wordplays in Polish memes

It is possible to note numerous instances of linguistic creativity in Polish Internet memes. Polish users make use of linguistic ambiguity, present contemporary content using obsolete forms of language, and juxtapose registers, similarly to creators of memes in English. The usage of intentionally incorrect spelling does not appear to be as extensive as the prevalence of LOLC at in English, which may be attributed to the fact that the relationship between spelling and pronunciation in Polish allows significantly fewer irregularities.

An interesting example of register juxtaposition could be the Internet meme about a well-known Polish linguist, Professor Jan Miodek.

Figure 7: "Professor Jan Miodek"

The template shows Miodek wearing a headset, in reference to a television programme where viewers of TV Polonia, a channel dedicated to bringing news and films to Polish people internationally, could call the professor via Skype and ask language-related questions. The text in the bottom panel aims to reveal the ambiguity of the text in the top panel; in this case, the town name *Stary Sącz* could be understood as an imperative "drink, old man" in a very informal register, and this is the sense which the dignified professor attempts to paraphrase on misunderstanding the question.

One of the examples of originality in Polish memes are the short, rhymed captions, very often superimposed on classical paintings or portraits of respected writers and historical figures as well as contemporary people and events. Due to constraints of the picture, the caption cannot exceed a set length, so the words and rhymes aim to condense the keywords related to the referenced person or phenomenon. The image below, from the satirical website zrymy.pl, features a portrait of Stefan Żeromski, a Polish novelist from the turn of the 20th century. The rhymed meme appears to juxtapose entertaining activities with the achievements of the figure. The literal translation of the caption could be "ladies, vodka, early spring, sadness, pain, a shattered pine", with "early spring" referencing the title of the novel, and "shattered pine" being one of the major thematic symbols in a different novel. Such a constrained, minimalistic form, which contains elements of poetry, may be used as an example of linguistic creativity specific to Polish users of memes.

Figure 8: A rhymed meme with Stefan Żeromski

Some Anglophone meme types relying on linguistic creativity have also been successfully transplanted into Polish. Among them is the Bayeux Tapestry meme, which features mock-archaic versions of familiar movie scenes. In the image below, a scene from a comedy *Dzień Świra* by Marek Koterski (*Day of the Wacko* in English) is represented using obsolete vocabulary and structures. In the scene, an irritated father berates his son for his poor progress in learning English.

Figure 9: Bayeux Tapestry meme in Polish

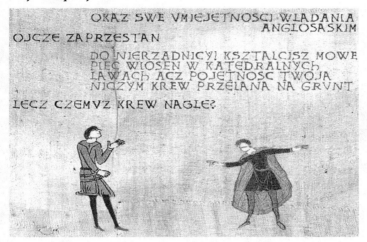

It may be worth mentioning that Internet memes are also propagated, replicated and might mutate in Silesian, a language or ethnolect characteristic of Polish Silesia, whose presence in memes may be perceived as a novel way of upholding regional norms and may present opportunities for further research. The examples below are replications of the "Story Time Jesus" Internet meme "featuring a painting of Jesus teaching a group of disciples with captions narrating gossipy, modern interpretations of famous Biblical narratives" (knowyourmeme.com). The Silesian version does not provide a literal translation but strives to convey the oral and informal character of Silesian; for instance, the sentence does not contain any expletives but it accurately renders the contrast between vernacular informality and the Biblical image.

Figure 10: Story Time Jesus in English and Silesian

It is to be noted that adopting a local language variety to render non-standard English is not a rule. Among translated memes, there are cases of both normalization (e.g. "Y U NO" templates in Polish closely adhere to target language rules of grammar and spelling) and of conscious introduction of non-standard features. For example, the meme "deal with it" has been translated into a consciously pidginized phrase that highlights the literal meaning of *deal* as "do business with" ("handluj z tym"), a non-standard feature that probably contributed to the meme's popularity in Poland.

Conclusions

Internet memes are exemplified in all their forms in Polish, starting from the simplest reaction faces and rage comics, both translated as well as original image templates, culture-specific memes, and conceptual memes. The use of non-standard linguistic forms is present. A certain preference for and popularity of the form of demotivational posters can be observed, which may be due to the success of demotywatory.pl. Internet memes are also created and propagated by the users of Silesian.

The analysis of case studies yielded the following conclusions. In terms of the image layer, it may be hypothesised that a close relationship between the background picture or a particular graphic artefact and the catchphrase or snowclone template increases the chance of the image being preserved and used ("Deal with it", "Y U NO") in a very similar form, with slight differences sometimes stemming from different generators imposing their own layout or font colour. Memes featuring culture-specific references are more likely to be significantly transformed in translation.

Internet memes may be viewed as a novel form of communication; they also act as carriers of cultural information. Through extensive use of linguistic creativity, non-standard forms of language and humour, Internet memes ensure their popularity and maintain users' interest. Non-Anglophone cultures adapt the known forms to their interests and produce a variety of templates. Very often, the target culture translates Internet memes into local standards, choosing acceptability over adequacy. Furthermore, groups that share interests may aim to propagate increasingly hermetic content.

There appear to be numerous research opportunities related to Internet memes. Studying the translation of Internet memes and their linguistic aspects allows to understand the mechanics of this novel form, hopefully allowing other scholars to further investigate this fascinating field.

References

Dawkins, Richard. 1989 *The Selfish Gene.* New York: Oxford University Press.

Gage, Cyle. 2007 http://cylegage.com/lulz, DOA March 5, 2013.

Pullum 2003, http://itre.cis.upenn.edu/~myl/languagelog, DOA November 4, 2013.

Toury, Gideon. 1995. *Descriptive Translation Studies and Beyond.* Amsterdam / Philadelphia: John Benjamins Publishing Company.

http://demotywatory.pl/4212990/Migdy-nie-bedziesz-tak-zajebisty, DOA November 4, 2013

http://www.reddit.com/r/movies/comments/1n43zq/fuck_it_im_getting_married_saturday_here_are_my, DOA October 30, 2013.

http://knowyourmeme.com, DOA May 1, 2013.

http://komixxy.pl, DOA October 8, 2013.

http://knowyourmeme.com/memes/story-time-jesus, DOA October 29, 2013.

Figures

Figure 1
http://i0.kym-cdn.com/entries/icons/original/000/002/252/me-gusta.jpg.
http://i1.kwejk.pl/site_media/obrazki/2012/01/7532f74235dc896a201501d2f7eb
fb53.jpg?1325626783.

Figure 2
http://i2.kymcdn.com/photos/images/newsfeed/000/140/938/responsibility
12(alternate).png.

Figure 3
http://i.imgur.com/VcibEQv.jpg.

Figure 4
http://demotywatory.pl/4218278/Zart-w-kawiarni-zapowiedzia-horroru, DOA
November 4, 2013.

Figure 5
http://komixxy.pl/faces/face_1340804044_by_Tabok.png.

Figure 6
http://fabrykamemow.pl/uimages/services/fabrykamemow/i18n/pl_PL/201111/
1321875599_by_ewciawawa_500.jpg?1321875599.
http://fabrykamemow.pl/uimages/services/fabrykamemow/i18n/pl_PL/201208/
1346357618_by_polak321_500.jpg?1346357618.
http://fabrykamemow.pl/uimages/services/fabrykamemow/i18n/pl_PL/201110/
1319662200_by_MusicLover_500.jpg?1319662200.
http://fabrykamemow.pl/uimages/services/fabrykamemow/i18n/pl_PL/201209/
1347310174_by_izyk85_500.jpg?1347310174.

Figure 7
http://komixxy.pl/uimages/201004/1272121887_by_kamilm123_500.jpg.

Figure 8
http://content.zrymy.pl/items/b/Q/bQNeM7Kcgm8w/31_zrymypl.jpg.

Figure 9
http://p.twimg.com/AqErOLFCAAAlbOL.jpg:large.

Figure 10
http://weknowmemes.com/wp-content/uploads/2012/03/story-time-jesus-
meme.jpg.
http://klopsztanga.eu/upload/20130718090118uid2.jpg.

Dominika Grygowska

Humour and cultural references in constrained translation. The Polish translation of *Munchkin*, a non-collectible card game

Constraints in the translation of card games

In their paper "Concept of constrained translation. Non-linguistic perspectives of translation" Mayoral, Kelly, and Gallardo created a table specifying the degree of constraints for various translations with more than one communication channel (1988: 364). Although card games were not incorporated in the table, their translation appears to require the preservation of similar kinds of synchrony as in the case of the comic, i.e. content synchrony and spatial synchrony. On each card, there is a combination of image and text which cannot be treated separately, as the image often constitutes part of the meaning or encourages the understanding of a given passage of text in a particular, often comical, way. A card may be viewed as a single-panel cartoon or as one frame of a comic strip. The translator should first consider each card as an independent unit, and then examine how this card can be related to the rest of the deck in order to avoid potential inconsistencies.

In *Munchkin,* the non-collectible card game which will serve as the case study for this paper, there are two types of cards, namely door cards and treasure cards. The most common cards in the former group are those with monsters and curses, as the name suggests, referring to what the players may encounter on the other side of the door. When it comes to the latter group, the most frequent cards represent various types of objects which can be used or worn by the players. Information visible on the cards may refer to the level of the monster in question, card title, technical description, the results of the player's defeat or success, bonuses and limitations of the object in question, object type and value. Taking into consideration the range of information derived by the player from the text on a card, the translator should include all instructions from the original, as any omission may influence the outcome of the game.

At the same time, because of the small size of cards, the translated text should occupy a similar amount of space. This spatial synchrony may become a problem because Polish translations are usually longer than English originals. Accordingly, the translator may have to decide whether to shorten or omit certain phrases in order to preserve the same print size and the size of the picture.

The picture itself is also a constraint which imposes limitations on the translators' choices. In *Munchkin* a number of card titles include visual puns, that is puns in which the image serves as replacement or addition to the meaning. For example, the title *Big Foot* is accompanied by the picture of a large foot rather than the mythical creature inhabiting the forests of North America. If this item was translated as *sasquatch*, the pun would probably not be understood by the audience. Apart from that, pictures may include references to the source text's culture. Thus, attention should be paid to possible associations connected with the picture, as an adequate translation needs to take into account the non-verbal elements of the card and preserve content synchrony.

Munchkin is a parody of RPGs and is aimed mainly at players able to understand these allusions; however, some of the puns or culture-specific items present in the game can be recognized by non-gamers as well. In general, all of the references can be grouped into two main categories, that is culture-specific and gaming- or fantasy-related references.

Culture-specific references

Munchkin can be described as a product of American culture, and more broadly, the shared Anglophone popular culture. Accordingly, in the ST, there are certain references which might not be understood and fully appreciated by the Polish audience. According to Antonini, culture-specific references connote "different aspects of everyday life such as education, politics, history, art, institutions, legal systems, units of measurement, place names, foods and drinks, sports and national pastimes" (2007: 154). For the purpose of this study, the category of cultural reference shall include all those references which are concerned with the outside world, that is people, places, objects, customs and events that exist or have existed in reality. For example, the title *Wight Brothers* refers to the Wright brothers, famous for constructing the first airplane.

When it comes to references to fictional characters, places, objects, customs and events, they too will be classified as a separate subcategory of culture-specific items, namely instances of intertextuality. The sources of such references include novels, poems, plays, advertisements or films. In *Munchkin*, since the actions, objects, and characters represented by the cards are a parody of role-playing games, many cards refer to fantasy-themed books, films or RPGs. This can be exemplified by the card titled *Mithril Armor*, referring to an object appearing in Tolkien's *The Lord of the Rings*, which is considered a cornerstone of the genre.

Many of these references involve puns and distortions. For example, the card title *The Chainsaw of Bloody Dismemberment* probably refers to *The Texas Chainsaw Massacre*. For the purpose of further analysis all such references to film titles, fictional events, characters, actors, and actresses shall be also included in the culture-specific group.

It is also to be noted that there may be two types of such references: specific and generic. Many references can be traced and attributed to particular texts; for instance, *Gelatinous Octahedron* is clearly a parodical version of a monster from the world of *Dungeons and Dragons*, and the relationship is confirmed by a similarity not only between the names of the creatures but also between the images. However, there are certain instances in which it seems difficult if not impossible to trace the source of a particular reference to a specific text. For example, *Munchkin* features fantastic races, such as elves and dwarves, which commonly appear in fantasy texts. It can be assumed that they do not necessarily refer to any particular type of creatures such as Tolkien's elves and dwarves, although Tolkien is certainly a major influence, but rather to the clichés the genre has collectively developed about them. Such generic references commonly include races, professions, certain monsters, potions and parts of equipment.

There are also cards which refer to various situations connected with pen and paper role-playing games which are not specific for any particular game but games in general. These references usually include behaviors which are characteristic of players or game masters and do not require theoretical but rather practical knowledge of the subject. The majority of such cases can be found in GUAL (Go Up A Level) cards, for example *Wash the GM's car*. It should be noted that the depicted situations cannot be defined as culture specific, but rather may be viewed as specific for RPG players' culture. They, too, may be assigned to the category of gaming- and fantasy-related references.

Humour, culture, and their interplay

Of the analysed 813 English-language *Munchkin* cards, as many as 270 include at least one element that can be classified as a (verbal or visual/verbal) wordplay or a cultural reference (defined as above). Given the numerous constraints, it is only to be expected that in some cases Polish translators will be able to preserve only some of the puns or cultural connotations. The purpose of the analysis is to determine what is usually lost in translation and which procedures are favoured by translators of *Munchkin*. However, before the results of analysis can be presented, a distinction between three groups of cards should be described.

Cards involving a pun only (i.e. without any culture-specific reference) may be represented by *Gazebo*, a card which features a picture of a gazing gazebo. The pun is based on the similarity in spelling of the two words. It is not a cultural reference, as such structures are present in the TC as well and have an already established name. The second type of card can be represented by *The Other Ring*, a card referring to Tolkien's *Lord of the Rings*: it features a cultural reference, but no wordplay. The third category, a mixture of a pun and a cultural reference, may be represented by a card called *Leprechaun*, showing a creature from Irish folklore suffering from leprosy.

Cards featuring wordplay only

The feature of *Munchkin* most valued by players is the sense of humour prevalent in the game. It would seem that preserving wordplays is a factor which may contribute to the positive reception of the product. The puns present in the game can be divided into monosemiotic and polysemiotic ones. If only one channel (verbal) is necessary for the pun to function it shall be classified as monosemotic, and when there is more than one channel (verbal and visual), it will be labeled as polysemiotic. Both types of puns are illustrated below.

Figure 1: Monosemiotic wordplay (on the left) and polysemiotic wordplay (on the right)

Zombees is a combination of the word *zombie* with the word *bees*. Although the pronunciation of *zombees* and *zombies* is the same, the spelling is different. Assuming that they do not treat this as an orthographic error, recipients can notice the double association without looking at the picture. Since the picture is not required, the pun can be classified as monosemiotic, although the translator always has to take the image into account. In *Fungus*, the spelling is not altered and the audience is not likely to understand the joke solely on the basis of the verbal channel. Here, the pun results from the similarity of the pronunciation of the first part of the word *fungus* – *fung* – to the word *fang*. The picture represents a mushroom with a set of fangs, and after seeing it the association becomes comprehensible to players. Since both visual and verbal channels are necessary for the *Fungus* pun to function, it should be classified as polysemiotic. By contrast, the wordplay present in the text below the picture, *Fungus was Humongous*, is monosemiotic. Overall, the group of cards featured 51 cases of polysemiotic wordplay, and 31 cases of monosemiotic wordplay. This tendency highlights the importance of images in creation of puns and shows that pictures and card names should not be treated as separate units.

Due to the fact that humour is an important part of *Munchkin* which contributes to its popularity, it was necessary to determine whether translators decide to preserve as many original puns as possible or use other solutions. All of the strategies applied by translators were classified in accordance with Delabastita's typology of procedures designed for translating humour:

Table 1: Translation of puns in cards containing wordplays alone

Procedure	No. of cases and percentage in the group
Pun → pun	34 (42%)
Pun → non-pun	23 (28.4%)
Pun → punoid	19 (23.5%)
Non-pun → pun	5 (6.2%)

The most frequently used procedure is pun → pun, appearing in over 40% of instances (34 occurrences), while the least common procedure is non-pun → pun, which was applied only 5 times. It seems that although translators at certain points attempted to compensate for previously lost puns, more often they decided to resign from double meanings (pun → non-pun, 23 cases, around 30%) or use a different rhetorical device (pun → punoid, 19 cases, over 20%). It seems that although humour is an important part of *Munchkin*, every second pun from this group was either lost or substituted by a punoid. On the one hand the data shows that half of the original puns were lost; thus, it may be assumed that preserving ST humour may be a difficult task for a translator. On the other hand, none of the analyzed puns were completely deleted (pun → zero). It appears that translators prefer – or perhaps are forced by the visuals – to retain at least one meaning of a pun or deliver a different humorous solution, rather than omit the whole passage. Later in this paper, these figures will be contrasted with ones related to those cards which also featured cultural references. First, however, some of the instances in which keeping puns seemed to be an especially challenging task or where the procedures used were especially interesting will be examined in more detail.

Pun → punoid

Examples of cards from this group may provide insight into the solutions invented by translators in situations when preserving puns from the ST seems either difficult or counterproductive.

The neologism *Pollyhedron* is based on the similarity of the word *polyhedron* and *Polly*, a name usually given to parrots. The picture represents a parrot made of a number of polyhedrons. In the TT, the card title became *Wielokostek*, which can be roughly translated as 'poly-dice' or 'poly-bones'. Although the name *Kostek* exists in Poland, it is neither particularly common nor associated with parrots. Thus, a reference to gaming dice is preserved, but the phrase ceases to be a wordplay and content synchrony with the image of the parrot is lost.

Grow Two Feet is a polysemiotic pun and is based on the literal representation of the phrase, that is a person with two extra feet. *Foot* is not used in Poland as a unit of measurement and the translator decided to use a neologism: *czterostopy*, which refers to the quality of having four feet. The TT does not carry the element of surprise which is present in polysemiotic puns.

In *Cross bow* the original pun was created by dividing *crossbow* into two separate words. Here, *cross* means 'annoyed' and, accordingly, the picture shows an angry bow. When it comes to the TT, in *Łuk Dwuręczny* (*two-handed bow*) the pun is no longer present. Since there are no one-handed bows, and all require the use of two hands, it seems that the translators attempted to create a humorous effect by stating the obvious. Again, the picture may be viewed as a constraint: the use of the adjective *dwuręczny* is not related in any way to the angry bow visible on the card.

Pun → pun

There are a number of card names consisting of one word, and it is usually an adjective. Most of these names describe certain qualities which may be added to monsters or parts of equipment if a given card is used by a player. One of such modifications which can be applied to monsters is *Miniature*, and the title can be both an adjective and a noun. The picture shows that the card causes a monster not only to be diminished in size but to literally transform into a miniature used in miniature wargaming. Although the Polish word *miniaturowy* is only an adjective, it has a similar set of associations, and thus the pun is fully preserved.

In *Cotion of Ponfusion* the pun is a spoonerism, based on replacement of the first letters of two words, that is *potion* and *confusion*. Although there are not many puns of this type in *Munchkin*, they appear to be relatively easy to translate. The pun is monosemiotic, and the picture itself cannot be viewed as a constraint that would hinder the translation process. The TT is *Zapój Namieszania*, and similarly to the ST, the positions of the first letters of *napój* and *zamieszania* were exchanged.

The pun in *Missile Toe* is based on the similar pronunciation and spelling of *missile toe* and *mistletoe*. The card shows a pair of red boots, which can be associated with Christmas, and two rockets protruding from the boots in the place where human toes should be. In Polish the whole phrase was translated as *Świąteczne Bombki*. Here, the pun is based on the similarity of the Polish words *bomba* (a bomb) and *bombka* (a Christams bauble, or a diminutive form of *bomba*). Although in the ST the pun was monosemiotic, as the audience could notice the surprising spelling of the phrase even without any input from the picture, in the TT the pun is polysemiotic.

Non-pun → pun

In *Monsters Are Busy*, the picture shows three creatures playing *Munchkin* and the situation rather than the card name may be perceived as a sufficient source of humour. However, in the TT it becomes *Potworna Partia Munchkina*, which offers the audience a double meaning. The word *potworna* is an adjective which implies that something is mostrous, i.e. terrible and cruel. The picture indicates that, here, *potworna* acquires a second meaning, namely it refers to the fact that game is being played by actual monsters.

Skull helmet simply denotes a headgear made of a skull, and this is exactly what the picture shows. The Polish translation, *Oldskullowy Hełm*, may be classified as a pun featuring a rare combination of the English word *skull* and Polish *oldskulowy*, from the English adjective *old school*, which means "[h]aving or adhering to old-fashioned values or ways" (http://www.oxforddictionaries.com/), a borrowing whose popularity in Poland is connected with the emergence of hipster culture.

Foot-Mounted Mace is a roundabout way of describing a ball and chain, a device worn by prisoners in the past, and this device is present in the picture. The Polish phrase *kula u nogi* refers to something or somebody who is a burden although it also means a ball and chain attached to a prisoner's leg; thus, *Kula u Nogi* can be classified as a pun.

Cards featuring cultural references only

This category includes cards with culture-specific items of various origin. Since it is not always possible to exactly determine the source of a given card name, the explanations should be treated as assumptions. Procedures applied by translators are divided in accordance with Aixela's typology of procedures devised for the process of translating culture-specific items (Aixela 1996). In cases where third culture references are present in the ST they will also be classified as usual cultural references. When an item from the ST culture is replaced with an item from a third culture, the translation will be labeled as autonomous creation, a procedure which is open for unconventional solutions. Only those references that may be perceived by Polish players as belonging to a foreign culture will be classified as culture-specific; for instance, all generic references to Christmas customs which are well-known both to the ST and the TT audience shall not be considered to be culture-specific items.

Table 2: Procedures used in translation of cultural references

Procedure	No. of cases and percentage in the group
Repetition	7 (6%)
Orthographic adaptation	2 (1.7%)
Linguistic (non-cultural) translation	38 (32.2%)
Synonymy	1 (0.8%)
Limited universalisation	10 (8.5%)
Absolute universalisation	20 (16.9%)
Naturalisation	21 (17.8%)
Autonomous creation	19 (16.1%)

A total of 118 cards featured cultural references only (as opposed to cultural references combined with wordplay). The most common procedure in translation was linguistic (non-cultural) translation (32%), and the least common choices were repetition, orthographic adaptation, and synonymy. Aixela divided the procedures into ones which promote the ST culture and those which promote the TT culture. Procedures focusing on preserving the ST references were used for around 40% of all card names from this group, which means that about 60% of the titles were subject to various degrees of domestication. It would seem that the translators decided to choose procedures which could transform cultural references into items that the TT audience find more familiar. Although linguistic (non-cultural) translation, which promotes the ST culture, was used most often, such instances were less numerous than the combined number of such procedures as absolute universalisation (17%), naturalisation (18%), and autonomous creation (16%). Nonetheless, there seems to be a tendency to either preserve the references from the source culture or provide references from the target culture, since absolute universalisation, which aims at depriving the TT of culture-specific items, was applied to only 20 cards. These figures will be later compared to those for cards which featured both cultural references and wordplays. First, however, examples of cards which underwent the most popular procedures shall be discussed in the following sections.

Linguistic (non-cultural) translation

Unspeakably Awful Indescribable Horror was translated as *Pradawne i Niewypowiedziane Zło,* which constitutes a reference to Lovecraft's works, with their purple prose and highly characteristic use of adjectives. The style of Lovecraft was preserved in the TT. Although specific phrases may not be direct citations from one particular work, the word choice indicates what author is being referred to.

Although the card name *The Other Ring* may not evoke associations with J.R.R. Tolkien's *Lord of the Rings,* the picture showing a ring from Peter Jackson's films causes the reference to be more noticeable to players. The situation is the same with its Polish counterpart, *Nie Ten Pierścień.*

Minor God may be similar to the previous example; the phrase seems to refer to *Small Gods* by Terry Pratchett. It features a picture of a small tortoise. In the novel, god Om is forced to take the form of this animal due to a crisis of divine powers. The TT, *Pomniejszy Bóg,* complies with the Polish translation of Pratchett's work, which is *Pomniejsze Bóstwa.*

It would seem that this procedure is applied by the translators when they assume that references in the ST references are familiar to players, and when there is an already established, fairly literal translation of a given term or phrase. However, on several occasions, despite the fact that Polish translations exist, different procedures are used.

Naturalisation

Fold, Spindle, and Mutilate means "to harm or disfigure" and refers to "a once-standard line printed on machine-readable documents" (http://idioms.thefreedictionary.com/). There was also a film *Do Not Fold, Spindle or Mutilate* from

1971 (http://www.imdb.com/). The card picture shows a stationery tool, spike, which is also called spindle, with three impaled orcs. Since in Poland there was no similar expression, translators provided a more familiar, musical reference, that is *Sztywny Pal Azji* (*hard pole of Azja*), where *hard pole* may be related to private parts, and where *Azja* is both a character from *Fire in the Steppe* by Polish writer Henryk Sienkiewicz and the name of the continent Asia. The phrase is a name of a Polish band, confirmed in an interview to have been selected for its various anatomical, geographical, and literary connotations (http://krakow.dlastudenta.pl/).

Short Wide Armor is related to a type of a vehicle, that is chevy short wide truck cars. It is an American product and its name is not that popular in Poland. With *Gdańska Zbroja Trzydrzwiowa* the car reference was replaced with a reference to a type of furniture called *szafa trzydrzwiowa* (*three-door wardrobe*) produced in the Polish city of Gdańsk. Both *short wide* and *szafa trzydrzwiowa* imply that the product has a large capacity. Furthermore, both of them are considered to be products clearly belonging to their respective cultures.

Although it may seem that the card *Narrow-minded* has no cultural connotations, it is the image that might be considered to present a character from the ST culture. The picture shows a stereotypical American clergyman, whose clothes and body posture may be viewed as not fully compatible with the image of a Polish priest. The TT card name, *Łojciec Dyrektor*, is related to the figure of father Tadeusz Rydzyk, known as Father Principal, who runs several highly recognizable, conservative Catholic media.

Absolute universalisation

M.T. Suit is related to the comic strips and TV series about Dilbert. M.T. Suit is a character looking like a walking suit without face or hands. He does not appear in the strips very often and is not recognizable to the Polish audience The translators decided to use a different solution and chose a culturally neutral phrase, *Widmo Biurokracji* (*Spectre of Bureaucracy*).

Katrina is a reference to the hurricane which struck the US in 2005 and, accordingly, the card shows a picture of a hurricane. Since Katrina was not covered in Polish media to a comparable extent, its name may not be recognized by most of the players. The Polish card name, *Oko Cyklonu* (*Eye of a Cyclon*), does not refer to any particular culture and is just a generic name of a weather phenomenon.

Curse! I Got a Rock is a reference to a phrase from an episode of the animated television series from 1966, *Peanuts*, titled *It's the Great Pumpkin, Charlie Brown*.

In this Halloween special, characters go from house to house, asking for sweets, and when they later compare what they had received, Charlie Brown always says: "I got a rock", a sentence which later became a catch phrase. The phrase is supposed to be used to reflect disappointment, and accordingly, the *Munchkin* card image shows two happy characters with bags full of gold, and one standing aside, holding a rock. While the TV series is not known to the TT audience, the comic strip, *Fistaszki*, is more popular; however, the only recognizable character is likely to be Snoopy. Thus, the Polish card name *Klątwa! Masz Kamyczek* (*Curse! You Get A Rock*) does not evoke associations with *Peanuts*, since the phrase itself has not been officially translated yet. The result is absolute universalisation.

Autonomous creation

Frost Giant can be a reference to Norse mythology or to characters from Marvel universe comic books and cartoons about the Avengers. The source of humour is the picture, which does not present a terrifying creature but a large snowman. Since Frost Giants may not be familiar to the majority of players, translators changed the card's title to *Bólinek*. This is related to an animated television series for children, *Bouli*, produced in France and broadcast in Poland under the title *Buli*, which at the same time is the name of the main character, a snowman. The translators replaced *bul* with its homophone, *ból* (*pain*), which would fit a dangerous monster. It is an instance of replacing an SC element with a third culture reference which can be more familiar to the TT audience.

Cheat With Both Hands is not a culture-specific item. It exaggerates the idea of cheating, which complies with the idea of being a munchkin. However, the TT *Wielki Szu* is a specific reference to a Polish film from 1982 under the same title, about an old cardsharp and his disciple. It appears that the use of autonomous creation constitutes a way to compensate for cultural references which might have been lost in other cards.

Autonomous creation was used for both *Vorpal Blade* and *Jabberwock*; however, the results are different. The two names constitute references to Lewis Carroll's poem "Jabberwocky", where Jabberwock is a monster and the vorpal sword is a weapon used to defeat it. Due to a large number of neologisms, the poem offers a challenge that has been undertaken by a number of Polish translators. There are several Polish renderings, each of them offering a different variant for both Jabberwock and the vorpal blade. The Polish card names are *Vorpowe Ostrze* and *Dżaberłok*, apparently unrelated to any existent literary rendering. Since *Dżaberłok* has similar pronunciation to *Jabberwock*, it may be recognized by those Polish players who are familiar with Lewis Carroll's works.

However, this does not apply to *Vorpowe Ostrze*. It may seem that since the translator decided to provide their own version of *Jabberwock*, they attempted to do the same with the other term, especially that the phrase used in existing Polish translations of the poem is different from the one in the card. The more probable explanation, which appears to be confirmed by the translation of the rest of the text present in *Vorpal Blade*, is that the translators may have failed to notice the connection between the two cards. The description explaining the use of the item reads: "An extra +10 against anything that starts with the letter J", where "J" is a reference to *Jabberwock*. However, the Polish translation reads: "Dodatkowe +10 przeciwko wszystkiemu co zaczyna się na literę 'S'", where "S" cannot be a reference to *Dżaberłok*, since it starts with a "D". The translation may result from the fact that *Jabberwock* comes from *Munchkin 2: Unnatural Axe* set, and *Vorpal Blade* comes from *Munchkin 3: Clerical Errors II*. Since usually a different group of translators work with each set, it may have been difficult to notice the connection, and this may have led to the oversight. Still, it is an isolated case, and it seems that when it comes to other cards, translators were aware of the sources of intertextual references.

Other procedures

Among less common procedures there were: limited universalisation (10), repetition (7), orthographic adaptation (2), and synonymy (1). Repetition was usually applied to names which funtion as borrowings in Polish, for example *Telemarketer* or *Teleport!*, as well as proper names, for instance *Kali* or *Krampus*. When it comes to limited universalisation, one of the interesting cases is *Lord Yahoo*, which became *Lord Bill*, with the original reference substituted by another Anglophone name.

Combination of wordplay and cultural references

Card names from this group feature both puns and cultural references. The aim of the analysis was to determine whether preserving humour was more important to translators than preserving cultural references. Although the number of such cards was not very high (75), certain conclusions can be drawn from the analysis. Most frequently both cultural references (from TT, ST or third culture) and puns or punoids were present in the TT (48%). Thus, it may be assumed that translators attempted to preserve both humour and culture if possible. In over 20% of card names only puns or punoids were present, and in 12% of card names only cultural references were retained.

Table 3: Frequency of preserving puns and references

References and puns in TT	No. of cases and percentage
Pun/punoid and cultural reference present in TT	36 (48%)
Only pun/punoid present in TT	16 (21.3%)
Only cultural reference present in TT	9 (12%)
Neither pun/punoid nor cultural reference present in TT	14 (18.7%)

It would seem that the translators showed a slight preference towards preserving humour rather than culture-specific items. This complies with the statement of Daria Pilarczyk, a representative of the Polish company translating and publishing *Munchkin*, Black Monk Games, that a considerable part of *Munchkin*'s popularity is based on its humour, and it is counterproductive to preserve those culture-specific items which could not be appreciated by Polish players (Pilarczyk 2014).

Ghost In The Shell is related to the Japanese manga, TV series, and animated science fiction film released under this title in the USA. The picture shows the ghost of a turtle with a headband, which may be a reference to American comic book and TV series titled *Teenage Mutant Ninja Turtles*. It would seem that in the card there are two cultural references; however, in the TT only one of them remains. The Polish card name *Wojowniczy Żółw* is a shortened version of the full title of the latter series. While at least one culture-specific item is still present in the TT, the pun is lost, which is one of the rare instances where preserving a cultural reference proved to be more important or simply more practicable.

The pun in *Curse! Yule Be Sorry* may be related to the Christmas episode of the animated TV series *Pinky, Elmyra, and the Brain: Yule Be Sorry*. Although the TV series and the said episode were aired in Poland, the TT *Klątwa! Wesołych Świąt (Curse! Merry Christmas)* cannot be viewed as a cultural reference since the title of the episode in Polish was *Smutne Święta* ('Sad Christmas'). In this situation both the cultural reference and the pun are lost.

In one case the Polish translation does not seem to be as successful as with the other card names. *Poultrygeist* is based on the similarity of the word *poultry* with the first part of the word *poltergeist*. The picture shows a ghost of a chicken which is throwing a brick. Apart from that, a film called *Poultrygeist: Night of the Chicken Dead* was released in 2006 and its name indicates that there may be some connection between the card name and the film. Although the Polish title of the film is *Poultrygeist: Noc Kurczęcich Truchel*, the translators decided to preserve the pun and create a combination of two words, namely *kura (chicken)*, and *straszydło (fright)*, which resulted in *Kurszydło*. However, it would seem that this pun is not as transparent as its ST counterpart. Apart from the fact that *straszydło* does not necessarily need to be a ghost, let alone an object-throwing poltergeist, the neologism seems more connected with the Polish word *szydło* (*awl*) and at first may seem inconsistent with the picture.

Cultural references versus humour: a summary of procedures

As presented in Table 1, for cards featuring only cultural references, the most frequently applied procedures were linguistic (non-cultural) translation (32%), absolute universalisation (17%), naturalisation (18%), and autonomous creation (16%). However, for cards featuring both cultural references and puns, it was also important to preserve humour, hence the differences in the use of particular procedures:

Table 4: Translation of culture-specific items in cards featuring both cultural references and wordplays

Procedure	No. of cases and percentage
Repetition	2 (2.7%)
Linguistic (non-cultural) translation	11 (14.7%)
Limited universalisation	6 (8%)
Absolute universalisation	28 (37.3%)
Naturalisation	15 (20%)
Autonomous creation	13 (17.3%)

As seen in Table 4, tn this latter group, the most frequently used procedure was absolute universalisation (37%), and the other common procedures were naturalisation (20%), and autonomous creation (17%). The data seems to imply that preserving the references was not as important as in the group of cards with culture-specific items only. Here 15% of card names were the subject of linguistic (non-cultural) translation while in the previous group it was 32%. Furthermore, even if the translators decided to keep a reference in the TT, it was subject to naturalisation or unconventional solutions. Since the ratio of procedures used in translation of card names with cultural references differs from that used for card names with both puns and culture-specific items, it can be assumed that one of the reasons may have been the necessity of preserving humour, which is the main strength of *Munchkin*. Hence, the frequency of procedures used for translating puns should be similar as in the case of card names with puns only.

Indeed, there is marked similarity between results in these two groups. When it comes to card names with puns only, the most popular procedures were pun → pun (42%), pun → non-pun (28%), and pun → punoid (23.5%). Apart from that, for five Polish card names a pun was created although there was no pun present in the ST. For cards featuring both cultural references and wordplays, the most frequently used procedures were pun → pun (40%), pun → non-pun (31%), and pun → punoid (24%). Non-pun → pun was used four times.

Table 5: Procedures used for the translation of puns: comparison between groups of cards

Procedure	Cards with both cultural references and wordplays	Cards with wordplays only
Pun → pun	30 (40%)	34 (42%)
Pun → non-pun	23 (30.7%)	23 (28.4%)
Pun → punoid (related rhetorical device)	18 (24%)	19 (23.5%)
Non-pun → pun	4 (5.3%)	5 (6.2%)

These numbers show that the distribution of procedures is similar to that observed in the translation of card names with puns only. This result may have been achieved at the expense of culture-specific items, since over a third of the renderings no longer featured any cultural references.

Localized cards

Preserving cultural references and puns at the same time was not always possible. The task may have been more difficult with card names which included both puns and cultural references. Some cultural references function both in the ST and in the TT culture; however, there are instances where a given item is too unique to be preserved in the TT. In such situations translators may apply naturalisation, limited universalisation or autonomous creation. Still, there are some cards for which even the application of these radical procedures may not yield a satisfactory effect. Then, a need to introduce one more, different solution may arise, that is modification of the picture itself or even creation of an entirely new card which is not present in the original set.

It would seem that there are various degrees of such localization in *Munchkin*. While radical changes include the deletion of whole cards or creation of new cards, the more moderate modifications may involve the modification of the picture, change of a colour or pattern, or the translation of text featured in the picture. The degrees of localization may be specified as follows:

1) 1st degree – translation of text featured in the picture;
2) 2nd degree – change of colour or pattern;
3) 3rd degree – modification of a small part of a picture;
4) 4th degree – deletion of original cards or creation of new cards.

In the next section the difference between these four types will be described in more detail and examples from each category will be provided.

Before any examples are listed, it is important to stress that some differences between the Polish and American versions of the cards occur regardless of translation decisions. The shade of colour is slightly different and the quality of the material from which the Polish cards are made is better. According to Daria Pilarczyk, the thickness of material results from the fact that Polish editions of *Munchkin* are printed in Poland, and not in China, as is the case with Steve Jackson Games. This is connected with the fact that Polish customers may have higher expectations regarding the quality and durability of the products. The layout of the texts and images on cards is also different to some extent: while in the American versions the text usually surrounds a picture, in Polish cards text is divided into blocks situated both above and below the picture. This results from the specificity of Polish language where words are often longer than their English counterparts. As a result, graphic designers have to change the font in order for the full text to fit in the space of a card.

When it comes to changes introduced to localize the content of some cards, the most frequent type of localization is that of the first degree, as there are 62 cards which feature translated text in their images. However, on several occasions despite the fact that a picture included a string of text, it remained untranslated in the Polish version. Some of these texts only consisted of numbers and did not require translation, and some could be understood by Polish players without a translator's intervention. For instance, the word *playtroll* remained unchanged, as it is a reference to a magazine published both in Poland and the USA under the same name, *Playboy*.

When it comes to modifications of images, there are certain rules which the Polish distributors of *Munchkin* must follow, and which are likely to become more strict in the future. According to Daria Pilarczyk, until now major changes of images have had to be accepted by Steve Jackson Games, and any additional card had to be drawn by *Munchkin*'s official artist, Kovalic. Although the cost of obtaining such picture is large, over 100 dollars, Polish distributors were willing to do so because such cards caused particular sets to be more attractive to players. However, there is a tendency in Steve Jackson Games to produce more unified sets of cards across different countries. It would seem that the aim of the creators of *Munchkin* is globalization and internationalization, rather than localization. All decks should have the same number of cards without "country-specific" pictures. The translation is not expected to be literal but it would seem that text will soon be the only area where any local flavour can appear.

Cards with the fourth degree of localization

Among the cards which were created specifically for Polish editions, most are directly related to characters and events from the target culture. Apart from that, there are puns which could be difficult to translate just as some puns from the ST are difficult to insert into the TT.

A card directly connected to the Polish political scene is *Lech, Czech i Jarosław*. The name itself is a variation of a title of a legend "Lech, Czech i Rus", describing the origins of three Slavic nations. In the card the name *Rus* is replaced by *Jarosław*, which together with *Lech* refers to two Polish politicians, the twin brothers Lech and Jarosław Kaczyński, who held the posts of Poland's President and Prime Minister, respectively. The card featuring two identical short individuals was issued in *Munchkin 1.6. Kości Zostały Rzucone* in March, 2009, shortly before Lech Kaczyński's death in a plane crash.

Another card, *Dwa Nagie Miecze*, is related to one of the most famous battles in Polish history, that is the battle of Grunwald, and the event which was supposed to take place shortly before the fight. The Grand Master Urlich von Jungingen, tired with waiting for the Polish-Lithuanian troops to begin the attack, sent to the union king, Władysław Jagiełło, two swords which were supposed to encourage him to start the battle. *Nagi miecz* means a sword without a scabbard, but it may also mean "naked". That is why in the picture a fig leaf is placed in the middle of each sword, as if to cover male genitals.

It would seem that in some cases there is a continuity between the localized cards. A good example are *Wieśmin* and *Wieśmin II Zabójca Knurów*, which refer to successful Polish video games *Wiedźmin* and *Wiedźmin 2: Zabójcy Królów*. Both games were translated into English, as *Witcher* and *Witcher 2: Assassins of Kings*, respectively. Both the card names are puns: *Wieśmin* is a combination of the word 'wiedźmin' and 'wieś', and accordingly the picture shows a character from the game holding a pitchfork. The second card, instead of 'Assassins of Kings', reads 'Assassin of Hogs'.

Since *Munchkin* is a parody of RPGs, in some of the localized cards there are references to games of this type which are either Polish or known to the audience, for example *Talizman z Magdą i Mieciem* or *Dzika Pola*. *Talizman z Magdą i Mieciem* shows a talisman with two portraits on it, one showing a man and the other a woman, since 'Magda' and 'Miecio' are Polish names. However, the whole phrase is primarily related to the board game *Talisman: Magia i Miecz* (original British name *Talisman: The Magical Game Quest*). The Polish edition of the game had its own artwork, which by some was considered to contribute to the specific atmosphere of the game or even cause the Polish edition to be better than the original. It also refers to a Polish magazine devoted to RPGs, *Magia i Miecz*, published from 1993 to 2002.

Dzika Pola, in turn, is a reference to a Polish pen-and-paper RPG. *Pola* is a female name, and the literal translation of the card title would be 'wild Pola'. The phrase also alludes to Dzikie Pola (Wild Fields), a historical region in the central Ukraine whose name appeared in documents from sixteenth to eighteenth century, and a Polish pen-and-paper RPG set in this period of time. Combining the two meanings, the card image shows a woman who, based on her outfit, is one of the winged hussars, a type of cavalry which contributed to Polish victories during that period.

Although there are more cards created specifically for Polish editions of *Munchkin*, some of the cards which were removed should also be analyzed. One of them is *Sword of Slaying Everything Except Squid*, which is linked with a card from an earlier deck, *Squidzilla*. The information below the image reads: "Does not give any bonus against Squdzilla. If you have this sword in play and encounter Squidzilla, you *must* try to Run Away!" The picture shows a sword with a small picture of a squid encircled by a prohibition sign on its grip. Since in the Polish edition *Squidzilla* became *Potwór z Bażin*, a cultural reference to a popular Czech song, there is no longer any connection to actual squids. In order for the card to function and be consistent with the previous translation, the image of the sword grip would need to be changed as well. It would seem that in order to avoid unnecessary modifications the publishers decided to remove the card.

Another card which was not included in the Polish edition of the game and which may have been omitted due to the possible interactions with a previously translated card is *Fowl Fiend*. It is a strong monster in the form of a chicken with a Cthulhu puppet on its wing, which can be easily defeated if the card *Curse! Chicken on Your Head* was used on a player. The picture this time was not drawn by Kovalic but Jonathan Rosenberg, the author of webcomic *Goats*, starring a chicken called Diabolo. However, in the Polish edition the chicken became a mohair beret, which is a pejorative reference to Polish Catholics who follow Father Rydzyk. Thus, there would be no connection between the word *fowl* and *mohair beret*. Apart from the fact that interaction between two separate cards would be lost, another issue which may have contributed to the omission of the card is the fact that the Rosenberg's webcomic is unlikely to be known to the target audience.

Another omitted card is *The Snerks*, whose name may refer to the American cartoon *The Snorks* about underwater creatures, and whose picture may be related to *The Smurfs*, a comic strip series created by Belgian artist Peyo, which later became a TV animated series. The card picture shows a red female snerk smoking a cigarette, wearing heavy make-up and fishnet stockings, while a male snerk is holding a blood-stained dagger and a pike with a human head on top of it. While *The Smurfs* were popular in Poland as a TV program for children, *The Snorks* are rather unknown to the audience. This may be the reason why the translators or publishers decided not to include the card in the Polish edition of *Munchkin*.

Survey: degrees of localization

In order to assess the target audience's attitude to the various types of localization, a survey was devised where they could opt for one of several translation solutions involving heretofore untranslated Munchkin cards, some of the options involving localization of the image. In every case respondents could also offer their own solutions. The questionnaire was conducted by means of an online form among *Munchkin* players, people generally interested in fantasy, and English philology students. There were two rounds of the questionnaire. During the first round it was available via link sent to senior English philology students, as well as internet forums. During the second round, thanks to the courtesy of the Polish publishers of *Munchkin,* the link was added on the *Munchkin* Facebook page.

In total there were seven cards for which the respondents were asked to choose the most suitable Polish version of those proposed, or provide their own ideas. In one case the card featured a wordplay, but not a cultural reference, and will not be included in the analysis. Extreme care was taken to generate options of comparable quality; in one case, the author's interpretation of the pun might have, in hindsight, influenced the answers, although they do not contradict the overall results. This case will, too, be excluded from analysis. Answers concerning the remaining five cards shall be discussed in following sections.

Results for *Spike the Egg Nog*

The card called *Spike the Egg Nog* includes a ST cultural reference to the common type of drink associated with Christmas. The image shows a character holding a large bottle with "xxx" written on it, dripping yellowish liquid. One drop is about to fall into a bowl standing on a table. The possible answers can be found in the Table 6 below.

Table 6: Respondents' answers for the card Spike the Egg Nog

Translation	No. of choices and percentage of respondents
Egg Nog	20 (6.1%)
Jajeczny Napój Świąteczny	108 (32.8%)
Po Jednym	131 (39.8%)
Others	70 (21.3%)

Most of the respondents chose *Po jednym* (40%) and *Jajeczny Napój Świąteczny* (33%), which means that in this case they preferred the card name to be more connected with the Polish culture or no specific culture at all. When it comes to the respondents' own solutions, the most commonly applied procedures were naturalisation (40%), autonomous creation (31%), and absolute universalisation (17%). It may be assumed that the majority of the respondents decided to translate the term so that it would have closer links with the TT culture, providing such translations as *ajerkoniak, poncz, kogel mogel* or various expressions connected with the drinking culture, for example *z prądem*.

Results for *Buckler of Swashing*

Buckler of Swashing includes a cultural reference and a pun created by dividing the word *swashbuckler*, so that it becomes an item they might use. The image represents a swashbuckler (a term with no ready Polish equivalent) holding a buckler and a sword.

Table 7: Respondents' answers for the card Buckler of Swashing

Translation	No. of choices and percentage of respondents
Puklerz ciachania	136 (41.3%)
Obciachowa tarcza	126 (38.3%)
Szpada nie lada	38 (11.6%)
Others	26 (7.9%)
No answer	3 (0.9%)

The most common answers were *Puklerz ciachania* (41%), and *Obciachowa tarcza* (38%). The structure of "Puklerz ciachania" (something of something) is commonly found in the names of RPG equipment and it would seem that the literal translation which closely reflected only one meaning of the original pun was slightly more popular than a card name variant which actually included a pun.

When it comes to the respondents' own translations, out of 26 propositions 7 included a pun, and 12 of them had references to the character holding the buckler but they did not include culture-specific items.

Results for *Christmas Goose*

Christmas Goose is a reference to a traditional type of dish served during Christmas. The picture shows the said goose with a halo over its head holding in its beak a scrap of material bitten off from the pants of Santa Claus, who is standing next to it. However, in Poland the dish most strongly associated with this winter holiday is carp.

Table 8: Respondents' answers for the card Christmas Goose

Translation	No. of choices and percentage of respondents
Świąteczna Gęś	171 (52%)
Gęsina na Św. Marcina	64 (19.5%)
Ciężkostrawny Obiad	49 (14.9%)
Others	42 (12.8%)
No answer	3 (0.9%)

As many as 52% of the respondents chose *Świąteczna gęś*, a literal translation which refers to the ST culture. A translation strictly related to the Polish culture was selected by 20%, and a neutral translation was selected by 15% of the respondents. 13% of them provided their own solutions, and the most frequently applied procedure was naturalisaton with 31 answers. It would seem that although the majority of respondents selected the variant including a reference to the ST culture, in situations where they decided to provide their own ideas they would mostly use domesticating procedures.

Results for *Seven Year Lich*

Seven Year Lich includes both a pun and cultural reference. The card name is related to *Seven Year Itch* with Marilyn Monroe, a film known in Polish as *Słomiany wdowiec*. The picture shows a variation on the famous scene from the film in which Marilyn's white dress is lifted by the wind, featring an undead creature, which explains the word *lich*.

Table 9: Respondents' answers for the card Seven Year Lich

Translation	No. of choices and percentage of respondents
Słomiana Wdowa	98 (29.8%)
Nawiedzona Narzeczona	71 (21.6%)
Ś-licz-notka	134 (40.7%)
Others	22 (6.7%)
No answer	4 (1.2%)

The most frequently selected answer was *Ś-licz-notka* (41%) but *Słomiana Wdowa* (30%) and *Nawiedzona Narzeczona* (22%) were also popular. In this case it would seem that keeping a pun is more important than preserving a cultural reference. Still, some of the respondents would prefer for a culture-specific item to remain in the TT. When it comes to translations invented by the respondents themselves, it would seem that they preferred to keep the pun at the cost of losing or modifying the cultural reference; however, in this case the difference between the most frequently selected answer and the other ones is not as marked as with the previous cards.

Results for *Tannenbomb*

Tannenbomb is a cultural reference, this time to a third culture, and a pun. The name is related to the German Christmas carol titled "O Tannenbaum" ("O Christmas Tree"). The pun was formed by replacing *–baum* with *–bomb*. The picture shows a Christmas tree decorated with a bomb and a stick of dynamite, with a fuse at the top of the tree. Since in this case image modification would seem forced, there was no option involving changes in the picture.

Table 10: Respondents' answers for the card Tannenbomb

Translation	No. of choices and percentage of respondents
Tannenbomb	96 (29.2%)
Bombka choinkowa	179 (54.4%)
Świąteczny gadżet	20 (6.1%)
Others	26 (7.9%)
No answer	8 (2.4%)

The most frequently selected option was *Bombka choinkowa* (54%); however, a significant number of the respondents (29%) decided to choose *Tannenbomb* as their answer. When it comes to the respondents' own propositions, they most frequently offered translations involving puns on the word *bombowy*, for instance *bombowa choinka* or *bombowe święta*.

Overall results for picture modifications

Each time the respondents were asked to decide on the degree of modification of the visual content, most of them selected pretty conservative options which involved no change of the image. However, in the case of *Spike the Egg Nog*, *Seven Year Lich*, and *Christmas Goose* over 20% of the respondents opted for minor changes. This may indicate that a small degree of localization is a more popular option.

Conclusion

The constraints which may be connected with the translation of card games included space, image and content synchrony, since many cards had both monosemiotic and polysemiotic puns. In certain cases Polish distributors decided to create completely new and unique cards to replace some of the original cards that could pose translation problems, which may be perceived as an instance of localization.

The analysis of those cards where the translation challenge was a wordplay showed that the most frequently selected procedure was pun → pun (42%). When it comes to cards which included only culture-specific items, the most commonly selected procedure was linguistic (non-cultural) translation (32%) but in total around 60% of all of the cards were subject to various degrees of domestication. Regarding the results for the group of cards with both humour and cultural references, in 48% of the cases puns or at least punoids together with culture-specific items of some kind were present in the TT. There may be a slight preference for puns over cultural references; however, in order to arrive at definite conclusions, more data gathered from the analysis of other decks of cards would be required. In the group of localized cards, usually only text present in the visual content of the cards was modified but there were also 35 cards which were either removed from or created uniquely for the Polish editions. It would seem that in the future editions of the game there might not be any cards created specifically for the Polish market, since the tendency of Steve Jackson's Games is to sell decks which do not differ from each other in terms of the number of cards or their visual content.

After the analysis of the questionnaire, it appeared that the respondents were not that strongly inclined towards domestication or foreignization. They did not express a strong need to preserve SC or third culture cultural references, and their preferences are rather connected with the presence or absence of verbal humour. When it comes to modification of the visual content, most of the respondents decided to leave the picture intact (from 64% to 89%). This would mean that the possible modifications of cards are not viewed as necessary. However, around 20% of the respondents suggested minor modifications of the pictures.

References

Aixela, Javier Franco. 1996. "Culture-specific items in translation: On the cultural aspects of translation" in Roman Alvarez and Carmen-Africa Vidal (eds.) *Translation, power, subversion*, 52–78.

Alvarez, Roman and Carmen-Africa Vidal (eds.) 1996. *Translation, power, subversion*. Clevedon: Multilingual Matters.

Delabastita, Dirk 1996. "Introduction" in *Wordplay and translation. Special issue of the translator. Studies in intercultural communication* 2.2, 127–139.

Delabastita, Dirk (ed.) 1997. *Traductio: Essays on punning and translation*. Manchester & Namur: St Jerome Publishing.

Jackson, Steve 2013. *Munchkin*. Poznań: Black Monk.

Jackson, Steve 2011. *Munchkin 1.6: Kości zostały rzucone*. Poznań: Black Monk.

Jackson, Steve 2009. *Munchkin 2: Wielosieczny topór*. Poznań: Black Monk.

Jackson, Steve 2009. *Munchkin 3: Kardynalne błędy*. Poznań: Black Monk.

Jackson, Steve 2010. *Munchkin 3.5: Piętno śmierci*. Poznań: Black Monk.

Jackson, Steve 2011. *Munchkin 4: Rumaki do paki*. Poznań: Black Monk.

Jackson, Steve 2011. *Munchkin 5: Łowcy głów*. Poznań: Black Monk.

Jackson, Steve 2012. *Munchkin 6: Opętane lochy*. Poznań: Black Monk.

Jackson, Steve 2009. *Munchkin*, Austin: Steve Jackson Games.

Jackson, Steve 2012. *Munchkin 7: Cheat with Both Hands*, Austin: Steve Jackson Games.

Jackson, Steve 2010. *Munchkin 3: Clerical Error*, Austin: Steve Jackson Games.

Jackson, Steve 2010. *Munchkin: Marked for Death*, Austin: Steve Jackson Games.

Jackson, Steve 2010. *Munchkin: Waiting for Santa*, Austin: Steve Jackson Games.

Jackson, Steve 2010. *Munchkin: Santa's Revenge*, Austin: Steve Jackson Games.

Jackson, Steve 2010. *Munchkin 4: The Need for Steed*, Austin: Steve Jackson Games.

Jackson, Steve 2010. *Munchkin 5: De-Ranged*, Austin: Steve Jackson Games.

Jackson, Steve 2010. *Munchkin 6: Demented Dungeons*, Austin: Steve Jackson Games.

Mayoral, Roberto, Dorothy Kelly and Natividad Gallardo. 1988. "Concept of constrained translation. Non-linguistic perspectives of translation" in *Meta: Translators' Journal* 33, 356–367.

Oxford Dictionaries, www.oxforddictionaries.com, DOA September 10, 2014.

Pilarczyk, Daria. 2014. Private communication (interview).

Contributors

All the contributors, as well as the editor of this volume, are graduates of the Department of English in the Faculty of Languages at the Nicolaus Copernicus University in Toruń, Poland. Translation Studies entered the Department as an M.A. specialization in 2001, with the first M.A. theses produced in 2003. Since then, over a hundred B.A. and M.A. works have been defended in translation studies in what is now Translation Studies Unit within the Department. All papers included in this volume are based on such diploma research projects.

Aleksandra Borowska received her B.A. in 2011 for a work which analysed the treatment of H.P. Lovecraft's idiosyncratic style in Polish translations. Her M.A., defended in 2013, studied the Polish versions of Anglophone Internet memes and the treatment of the linguistic features which contributed to their popularity. The work featured a survey on the perception of translated and localized memes by Polish users. She is now working towards her PhD.

Natalia Grabowska received her B.A. degree in English in 2011, for a thesis on how cultural elements of the East, portrayed in Mickiewicz's poetry, were rendered for the Western readers, and how the Orientalizing literary devices, such as extended metaphors or epithets, fared in the two analysed translations. In 2013 she earned her M.A. with a study of register juxtaposition in the Polish translations of selected Shakespearian dramas.

Dominika Grygowska obtained her B.A. in 2012 and her M.A. in 2014. In her B.A. she studied the translation of proper names in fantasy novels, and in her M.A. she followed her interest in the under-researched topic of translation of card games. Apart from the analysis of several sets of cards, her work featured extensive interviews with game publishers and translators, and surveys of the player community. Currently, she works for a translation agency.

Karolina Retkowska obtained her B.A. in 2011. In her B.A. work, she analysed English translations of *Pan Tadeusz*, a work she personally admires as a masterpiece deeply rooted in Polish tradition. Her work featured a survey conducted on native speakers of English to check the reception of the various renderings. She went on to study British literature and received her M.A. in 2013.

Joanna Szakiel obtained her B.A. in 2011 with a study of ideological shifts in the translation of John Paul II's biography from English into Polish, and in the translations of press articles concerning the pope. Her M.A., defended in 2013, focused on self-translation and bilingualism, as described by linguists and translation scholars, and the self-perception of author-translators, illustrated with the analysis of three works by Gross: *Neighbors*, *Fear*, and *Golden Harvest*.

Ewa Tadajewska received her B.A. degree in 2011 and M.A. degree in 2013 from Nicolaus Copernicus University in Toruń. During her studies she became interested in translating children's literature. Her M.A. thesis discussed the ethics and ideology of rendering culture-specific items in translations for children, on the example of *Anne of Green Gables*. Since 2013 she has been teaching English in a language school.

Krzysztof Wadyński obtained his B.A. in 2011 and his M.A. in 2013. Interested in the history of Poland in the 17th century, in his B.A. he studied the translations of items unique to that region, and in his M.A. he anlaysed translation problems in the Polish translation of Niall Ferguson's *Empire* from the perspective of translator's competence.

Dis / Continuities
Toruń Studies in Language, Literature and Culture

Edited by Mirosława Buchholtz

Volume 1 Mirosława Buchholtz / Grzegorz Koneczniak (eds.): The Visual and the Verbal in Film, Drama, Literature and Biography. 2012.

Volume 2 Mirosława Buchholtz: The Beautiful and the Doomed: Essays on Literary Value. 2013.

Volume 3 Joanna Mstowska: Various Aspects of Mimesis in Selected Sea Novels of Frederick Marryat, James F. Cooper and Richard H. Dana. 2013.

Volume 4 Agnieszka Łowczanin / Dorota Wiśniewska (eds.): All that Gothic. 2014.

Volume 5 Mirosława Buchholtz / Dorota Guttfeld / Grzegorz Koneczniak (eds.): Henry James Goes to War. 2014.

Volume 6 Mirosława Buchholtz: Henry James and the Art of Auto/biography. 2014.

Volume 7 Tadeusz Sławek: Henry David Thoreau – Grasping the Community of the World. 2014.

Volume 8 Mirosława Buchholtz / Eugenia Sojka (eds.): Alice Munro: Reminiscence, Interpretation, Adaptation and Comparison. 2015.

Volume 9 Sławomir Wacewicz: Concepts as Correlates of Lexical Labels. A Cognitivist Perspective. 2015.

Volume 10 Dorota Guttfeld (ed.): Facets of Domestication. Case Studies in Polish-English and English-Polish Translation. 2015.

www.peterlang.com